The Germond Family Murders

A Forensic Conclusion to a Cold Case

Vincent Cookingham, Ph.D.

outskirts
press

The Germond Family Murders
A Forensic Conclusion to a Cold case
All Rights Reserved.
Copyright © 2022 Vincent Cookingham, Ph.D.
v4.0 r1.0

The opinions expressed in this manuscript are solely the opinions of the author and do not represent the opinions or thoughts of the publisher. The author has represented and warranted full ownership and/or legal right to publish all the materials in this book.

This book may not be reproduced, transmitted, or stored in whole or in part by any means, including graphic, electronic, or mechanical without the express written consent of the publisher except in the case of brief quotations embodied in critical articles and reviews.

Outskirts Press, Inc.
http://www.outskirtspress.com

Paperback ISBN: 978-1-9772-4761-2
Hardback ISBN: 978-1-9772-4824-4

Cover Photo © 2022 Vincent Cookingham, Ph.D.. All rights reserved - used with permission.

Outskirts Press and the "OP" logo are trademarks belonging to Outskirts Press, Inc.

PRINTED IN THE UNITED STATES OF AMERICA

Stanfordville, New York November 26, 1930
MURDER VICTIMS

James and Maybelle Germond, parents

Raymond Germond, 10, son

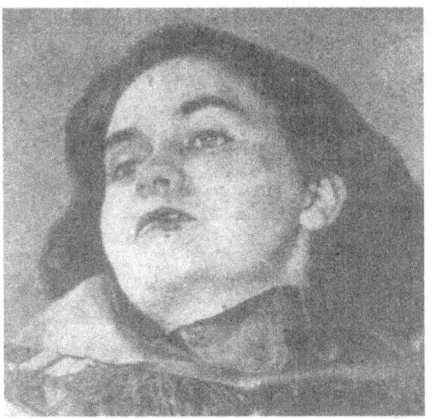

Bernice Germond, 18, daughter

Table of Contents

About the Author i
Introduction iii
1. The Great Coincidence 1
2. Stanfordville, New York 8
3. The Media and Rumors 21
4. Further Initial Case Observations 31
5. Trying to get All the Evidence 45
6. Court Victory 49
7. Conclusions & Acknowledgements 73
8-9ff. Explanations & Exhibits 82

Exhibits

Exhibit #		Page #
1A1, 1A2, 1A3	Family History	87-89
2A, 2	History	90–91
3	Stanfordville	92
4	Clinton Corners Store	93–94
5	Curry House	95
6	Creek View	96
7	Germond Side Kitchen	97
8	Knife Found area	98
9	Barn Yard – bodies found	99
10	Wagon Shed	100
11	Overview of area	101
12, 12A	Curry Photos	102–103
13	Newspaper on table	104
14	Gloves	105
15, 15A	Knife & Replica	106
16	Kitchen Door	107
17	Close up Kitchen	108
18	Open door - foot	109
19	Mrs. Germond - Stove	110
20	Kitchen both bodies	111
21	Both Female bodies	112
22	Bernice's body	113

Exhibit #		Page #
23	Raymond body- shed	114
24	Hay Cart	115
25	Bodies in Shed	116
26	Crowd at scene	117
27	Reward Poster	118
28	Curry's Prints	119
29	Curry Death Notice	120
30, 30A, 30B	Court Order	121–123
31	Letter from lawyer	124

About the Author

DR. COOKINGHAM HAS over 50 years of investigative and forensic science experience as a law enforcement officer, corporate executive, consultant and university professor in forensic science. He has numerous peer-reviewed professional publications and books.

He holds a Ph.D. with a doctoral dissertation in the forensic applications in white-collar crime. In addition, he holds degrees of Master of Business Administration and a Master of Arts from the John Jay College of Criminal Justice. Also a Bachelor of Science degree in Forensic Science and three Professional Board Certifications.

Dr. Cookingham is a veteran of the United States Marine Corps as well as a native New Yorker who currently resides in Port St. Lucie, Florida.

Introduction

THIS IS A true story of the multiple murders of a poor dairy farm family during the depression in upstate New York. The case went unsolved for 90 years. This awful crime has been reported worldwide throughout the years and has been the focus of a slew of amateur detectives over the years. It is routinely retold in annual newspaper articles promoting endless hypothetical theories, solutions and motives. Its memory has survived in crime mythology in the same manner as the "Jack the Ripper" case. By pure coincidence, I am the only professional with an extensive forensic background to have ever investigated this case and recovered whatever retained evidence remains. It was necessary to obtain a court order for all this evidence and receive the cooperation of District Attorney William Grady and other staff of the Dutchess County New York government.

But for the most incredible of coincidences in criminal investigatory history, the case would have remained unsolved.

This is the true story of that solution 90 years later and the truly incredible coincidence that provided that solution.

CHAPTER 1

The Great Coincidence

I THOUGHT THAT in order to tell this story properly, I should utilize the Casey Stengel rule: "the best place to start is at the beginning." County Roscommon Ireland, 1918. Twenty-two-year-old Margaret Fallon journeys by bus to the Port of Cork to board a ship for America. She wanted to start a new life and already had two sisters and a brother living in the New York State area. After the twelve-day voyage she arrived in New York City at Ellis Island and discovered immediately that it had no resemblance to the poverty of the rural farm land in County Roscommon. (Exhibits #1, ff) She always remonstrated that the Ellis Island process was humbling and to a large extent enervating. As a faithful Catholic, her first stop after her sister met her was to visit St Patrick's Church in Long Island City to give thanks for her safe arrival. (See Exhibits #'s 1A1, 1A2, 1A3)

Though the depression was ten years away, finding a job to support oneself was the most significant strategy pursued by a new legal immigrant. Margaret was no exception. She had some limited experience caring for babies in Ireland and fortunately she made a contact through her brother with a physician (Dr. Strong) in upstate New York in the small farming village of Stanfordville, New York. Dr. Strong had a very large house and estate in Stanfordville and resided with his large family. The estate had some small amount of farming with several milk cows and other livestock. Margaret was subsequently

THE GERMOND FAMILY MURDERS

interviewed and Dr. Strong hired her as a baby's nurse for his children. She became quite happy in this position together with a free residence on the estate. Dr. Strong had a number of employees including a part-time, 18-year-old farm hand named Russell Cookingham who worked for him in addition to his fulltime job on the family farm in Stanfordville.

Russell developed a relationship with Margaret and he was converted to the Catholic Church and in 1918 they were married at Immaculate Conception Catholic Church in the nearby hamlet of Bangall, New York. A relationship that lasted for over 50 years and the raising of nine children. The first three of which were born in Stanfordville. Then seeking a better life for his ever-growing family, Russell made a contact in New York City and was hired by Consolidated Edison that caused them to move from the farm to Astoria, Queens. All of the offspring went on to various careers and started families of their own including one son, John, who was killed in action on February 21, 1944 at the battle of Anzio, Italy. He received the Silver Star for "Gallantry in Action." Russell died in 1968 and Margaret died in 1975. The next to the youngest, Vincent, went on to a professional career in law enforcement and went on to become a consultant in forensic science while being appointed to the faculties of four universities and published numerous professional articles and several books. Vincent always loved his return to Stanfordville, Amenia and Pine Plains where he loved the farm work with his grandparents and the farms of Uncle Bevan and Aunt Ida. He considered this the happiest time of his childhood.

I can recall the sound of the rushing water of Wappingers Creek near my grandparents' home in Stanfordville. Making the milk rounds with my cousin on his milk truck was always a delight since we'd go to various farms to collect their milk. The taste of fresh milk from the coolers is still fresh in my remembrance. However, cutting hay in the hot sun was only fun for a little while. After he retired, my grandfather took a parttime job at the Stanfordville cemetery marking off the graves and digging many of them. He recruited me to hall small

THE GREAT COINCIDENCE

stones for him which he used to mark off the graves. I viewed myself as a very important person assigned to this task. As an irony with obvious notice, my family would later be buried at this location as well as the remains of the four victims of this horrendous crime that had occurred 25 years earlier. My grandmother would take me up the road to Ford Friedah's general store for cookies. I can clearly recall sitting beside Wappingers Creek and watching the vehicles pull in to Ben Wheeler's Feed Store. This same store exists to this very day as a residence. It had a history as not only a feed store but also a large hay barn and one of my relatives stored calves in there. The structure sits directly cross the road on Depot Lane from my grandparents' former home. I never realized that over 60 years later, I would be called upon to investigate one of the most widely reported multiple murders in the states' history as a cold case that happened two miles upstream from my family's residence in 1930. The aforementioned Ford Friedah was a sworn witness back in 1930 at the inquest hearing as he was one of the first group of people on the scene to help milk Germond's cows. The raw coincidences were building over the years and began to refresh my memory when I was assigned to this case. My uncle Harold was even a sworn witness at the inquest of these murders

As will be apparent later, two very prominent names in the settling of this area many decades ago were the families of "Germond" and "Cookingham." The later had their lineage in Germany where the name was "Guggenheim" that translated (roughly) into English as "Cookingham." It is believed that the family were devout Lutherans and Catholics (originally) and preferred to maintain their "Christian" identity. It is not at all surprising that most of the farmers raised the German style dairy cow known as the "Holstein." (See Exhibit #1) Moreover, my other relatives through marriage were families named Dykeman and Hoffman in surrounding areas such as Pine Plains and Stanfordville. My parents were married in Immaculate Conception Church in Bangall and several of the other siblings were Baptized there as well. The Church no longer stands.

Perhaps an act of fate would carry me back to the region from

THE GERMOND FAMILY MURDERS

my home in Port St. Lucie, Florida. While on a business trip to Poughkeepsie, New York, I sought out a pistol range where I could qualify with my handguns as I was required by law to do so once per year. As a retired police officer, I was given a federal license to carry a concealed weapon under Congressional Law established for that purpose. I examined local onsite listings and discovered that the Dutchess County Sheriff's Office maintained a pistol range and provided such requalification services so I immediately made an appointment and reported for the training. The date was sometime in the Spring of 2013.

The training was being conducted by Sergeant Jonathan Hughes, Records Officer, Dutchess County Sheriff's Office. "We had a long conversation and we became somewhat friendly. The talk came around to my last name: "Cookingham," a rather well-known name in Dutchess County with even several roads bearing the family name. The Sheriff of Dutchess County in 1933 was Oakleigh Cookingham, a distant relative as I am told. We started to chat about the famous murder case in Stanfordville in 1930 and Jonathan indicated that his office had preserved the original crime-scene photos and some sporadic reports. I believed that the evidence was too old and no scientific evidence would be available. However, since I had retired recently, I thought this a good opportunity to "give back to younger cold case investigators." So, I decided to make an appointment with Jonathan to come back and examine what was in his possession. I had heard of the case as a child but had no specific knowledge so I agreed to take a look at the retained evidence. On my return to the Sheriff's Office, I took high-intensity mobile phone pictures of the 22 photos and retained them for study and reviewed the existing memos. As Jonathan explained, these photos have been made available to countless media and newspaper personnel and have appeared in publications many times. So, you can imagine the amazement that I felt that as a forensic scientist I would be asked to examine a cold case that happened in 1930 within running distance of my family's home town where I played as a child.

THE GREAT COINCIDENCE

In order to familiarize myself with the case, I recovered as many newspaper articles and documentation as possible including the fine work of a local historian (I can't forget Ginny). I studied what had been given to me for the next year as time permitted. I recovered hundreds of pages of newspaper articles and international publications. This crime attracted world-wide attention in mystery publications. There were endless private investigator's notes and freelance writers who have opined on this case. I was unable to find the work of any qualified professional anywhere in the world who had examined the evidence. The photos, when compared to all this information revealed and entirely different scenario. An extensive critical evaluation of all this information will be found in my work that follows.

So, I embarked on my mission over the next couple of years and initially received very little cooperation from record keepers and other interested parties. I was told things like: "That case has been solved, he did it," and "You're wasting your time it happened so long ago," and "There's no DNA so we'll never know." If forensic scientists spent most of their time watching television, rarely would a case be solved.

A forensic scientist is rarely concerned with rumors, speculation, motives and reputation. A great clergyman once advised that "reputation is rarely proportioned to virtue." Actually, the forensic scientist is primarily concerned with scientific research and the physical sciences. For example, homicide can be divided into specific typologies:

1. Suicide
2. Murder for Hire
3. Revenge or rage killing and,
4. Murder in the furtherance of another crime.

Years of professional research on these typologies exist in the professional record and this is quite helpful to the forensic scientist in the initial evaluations. In other words, there are historic and provable fact-patterns that tend to occur in all of these types of events. Though a scenario may initially indicate a certain typology, the investigator should be alert to the clear possibility that more than one typology may exist. This is where the great skill comes in – one opines on knowledge guided by experience.

Moreover, one should never underestimate the influence of politics in major crimes that gain substantial attention and this case will prove to be no exception.

There's only one thing worse than politicians entering a case and it's when lawyers arrive. Some would argue with me about that and would claim it's the media entering when facts can become the occasions of chance. I always think of Mike Schmidt, the professional baseball player, who spent his whole career in Philadelphia with a tough press. Mike said when he retired that "playing in Philadelphia, where you can experience the thrill of victory and the agony of reading about it in the papers the next day."

As you will soon see, this case has all of the foregoing intervening variables.

However, in order to properly understand this case, it must be viewed in terms of different timeframes. First, the initial findings of the onsite investigators and the large volume of theories and media accounts that took hold during the period after 1930. Secondly, the reopening of the case in 1933 by then Governor Rockefeller. Thirdly, the evaluation of the actual evidence as a result of the court order granting me access to the autopsy files and all other documents as well as the inquest minutes. It is this evidence that put to rest the vast majority of the media accounts and rumors of the day.

Keep in mind that there was an accepted body of evidence prior to my investigation that was internalized for many years to come. It can easily be demonstrated by in-depth analysis and the use of scientific techniques, that a probative fact pattern could now be established. It was therefore in the scientific investigation of this case and contemporary techniques, that the solution of this case could reasonably be determined.

In the next chapter, the initial understanding of events that have survived for nearly 90 years was born and perpetuated by media, magazines, panel discussions and book authors. It is this great coincidence that enabled me to correct the record.

At the very end, what surprised me the most is that not a single publication, newspaper, media source or even the original investigative agency was willing to comment or even correct the record.

CHAPTER 2

Stanfordville, New York Before and After November 26, 1930

THE GREAT NINE Partners Patent in 1697 included the area of Dutchess County, New York that would later include the formation of the Town of Stanford including the two hamlets of Stanfordville and Bangall.

The idyllic setting as I remember it has changed somewhat but I can still remember the intersection of Rt. 82 and the Salt Point Turnpike. That intersection looks exactly the same as I remember it. The gas station is still up the road but in more modern format but I don't recall that location being known as "Curry's Corners" as referring to that intersection. Of course, my childhood memories occur about 25 years after the historic events that would take place there. I was filled with nostalgia during all of my inquiry never dreaming that I would return here someday in a semi-official capacity.

Bangall looks a great deal different. The Catholic Church is gone where my parents were married and where a number of my siblings were Baptized. I can still remember nearby Hunns Lake. An amusing event occurred during my inquiry. I came across an advertisement by a local merchant touting the tourist attraction in Bangall, New

York. One of the claims was that the world famous Germond Family Murders happened nearby. Somewhat of a poetic license as the crime scene cannot realistically be a tourist attraction for this case as it happened a few miles away. I wrote these folks a letter advising them of my investigation and of the slight exaggeration of the claim, which by the way, was not in bad faith. I never received a response. One of my great memories of Bangall was Bastonies Bar & Restaurant whereat an enormous painting of "Custer's Charge" at the Battle of Little Big Horn was prominently displayed and its beauty the subject of regular commentary. There were two men there once who advised me that the battle occurred right here in Bangall just down the road and with youthful ignorance I bought the story until I got back to New York and opened my history book and realized that these men were either ignorant or were just teasing me. I opted for the latter.

A trip to Pine Plains was necessary to continue visits to childhood sites. The Old Stissing House was still there though not as busy as it once was but the caretaker was kind enough to take me on a tour of the old place where meals are still served during limited weekday seating and there are no hotel guests any longer. While in Pine Plains, I travelled out a few miles to my aunt's old farm on Hoffman Road and found the barns and silo had been removed but the beautiful water fall at the beginning of Hoffman Road was still there as I remember it.

From Pine Plains I travelled back toward Bangall and took the Bangall-Amenia Road to where my other aunt and uncle tended to a farm on Pugsley Hill Road. Unlike other family members who raised Holstein dairy cattle, my uncle raised Guernsey Dairy Cattle. (See Exhibit#1, ff) My family in Stanfordville, Pine Plains and Amenia were the loveliest people that I have ever known. It saddens me that throughout the rest of my adult life, I was not able to stay in contact with them. I did see some of them from time to time. When I ended my day, I would always make a trip back to the Stanfordville cemetery to pay my respects to my family buried there and then go and sit in my car by the Creek near the Old Ben Wheelers Feed Store across from my grandparents' home going over the day's findings.

Recent residents of the vicinity of this crime refer to the site as "Clinton Corners." I know of no person during my childhood that would refer to this location as "Clinton Corners." It has always been referred to as Stanfordville since I believe it is still contained in the Town of Stanford.

Stanfordville, New York in 1930 was a rural dairy farming community of rather small farms in proximity to each other. The population of Stanford in 1930 was 1269 and most inhabitants resided in and about Stanfordville. It is located nearly 100 miles north of New York City in Dutchess County. The morning of November 26 was a rather cold day typical for that time of the year in this area with the 4:00 P.M. temperature at 22 degrees. The depression was in full impact in the area and if there was an advantage to dairy farming, it was in the farmer's ability to sustain themselves and have a constant source of meager income as well as raising their own food and other sustenance. It was a time of patched-together equipment, work horses and bartering, no toilets or running water, heat was supplied by wood burning stoves for heating and cooking. Of course, there was "the outhouse which in the winter time was about 10 yards too far and, in the summertime, it was about 10 yards too near." To say it was a small town would be an under statement. The 1930 population of the Town of Stanford was 1269 not counting the dairy cattle. People were quite familiar with one another in this area. A stranger didn't go unnoticed very long.

Milk was sold to the local Borden Creamery and most folks did business with Ben Wheeler's Feed Store near the creamery on now what is Depot Lane. As a personal note, my grandparents' house was across the road from Ben Wheeler feed store that used to be a hay barn right on the Wappingers Creek. Kitchen water pumps were used as well as the larger outside pump and electricity was by this time fully utilized including in the milk barn where the milking machines were now powered by electricity.

However, coal oil lamps were still fully in place. I can remember my dad pumping water in the morning and cutting kindling for the stove in the morning. My grandparents had long since given up the farm and moved into this old house which still stands in remarkably restored condition. I loved staying there and waking up in the morning to the sound of rushing water from the creek. I can also remember walking up the road with my grandmother to Ford Friedah's general store to pick up bottles of milk. Mr. Friedah had already testified in the inquest at the Germond Murders back in 1930; a fact that I would not come to realize until I undertook this investigation. I had only heard of passing comments about this horrible crime as a young boy and only on several occasions as I grew older. However, I do remember the many theories people still maintained even thirty years after the crime.

The following narrative is the "generally accepted scenario" of this horrendous crime with numerous variances over the years. I urge the reader to keep this in mind that much of the scenario surrounding this crime can be scientifically disproven as one will see. In addition, almost all writers on this crime merely repeated rumors and local newspaper accounts and regularly introduced unprovable speculation. In fact, in over five years of research, I was unable to locate a single professional criminal investigator and / or accomplished forensic scientist who had ever examined this case or its retained evidence. Moreover, there were writers who have actually gained fame by writing about this case without any knowledge of the facts and regularly produced information that could be scientifically disproven even on the retained evidence. Please then, do keep in mind that some of the reports in the very few newspaper accounts that I will cite here (I could have cited at least 100 more) contain disprovable information. The same can be said for other writers of articles and even books.

On the Salt Point Turnpike one quarter mile south of the County Road (Now rt. 82) lies the leased farm managed by James Husted Germond in February, 1930. (See Exhibit #26) He was not a well-to-do man and earned his living the only way that he knew just as his forbearers had taught him, as a dairy farmer. He was only milking about twelve cows at the time and, in those days, hardly an ideal target

THE GERMOND FAMILY MURDERS

for robbery. He resided there with his wife Mabel, 48, his daughter Bernice, 18, and his son Raymond 10. Mr. Germond was known to family and friends as "Husted."

Earlier on that November 26, Husted drove with Raymond to Millbrook where he cashed a milk check for $150 and paid a $50 feed bill as well as other bills. It should be noted here that later investigation would indicate that he actually cashed a check at the bank for $214.47 and received $154.43 in return. Furthermore, when he paid all the bills that day, he was left with approximately $69.00 which contradicts the 90-year reporting that he had about $90 when attacked. On the way home in midafternoon, he stopped at his brother Paul's farm about 2 ½ miles down the road from his own in the direction of Clinton Corners to grind grain and fill sacks.

On this cold Wednesday evening (Thanksgiving Eve), Mabel Germond was in her farmhouse in Stanfordville, readying for the Thanksgiving festivities with the family. As she worked in her kitchen, her husband Husted was outside attending to his chores allegedly with his 10-year-old son Raymond (Ultimately disproven by the facts). Their daughter Bernice was expected home on the bus at any time after attending a class at vocational training in Poughkeepsie and was in fact dropped off in front of her house at 5:20 P.M. It was dark and cold.

Husted did not deliver his milk to the Borden Dairy Co. Creamery in Stanfordville the next morning (Thanksgiving) and some people thereat thought: "At last Husted's taking a holiday!" He had never taken one before. But when he didn't appear on Friday, a cold wintry November 28, the dairy superintendent sent Willard Coons, a Borden employee to the Germond farm to determine why Husted had not delivered his milk. There was no one in sight in the Germond barnyard and no one in the cow barn where the cows "stood with swollen udders." He shouted a greeting as he walked to the wagon shed 150 feet away and the door was slightly ajar. He swung the door open and there before his eyes lay Germond and Raymond bloody from many knife wounds and frozen. (See Exhibit#25). It would have been clinically impossible at that moment for Mr. Coons to determine that what he saw were knife wounds – more later.

Coons raced by car to Paul Germond's farm, (about 2 miles south of the crime scene) and shouted as the car entered the barnyard "Husted's been murdered! Husted's been murdered!" Paul ran out of his house followed by his father-in-law George Rogers. As they ran Coon shouted "Raymond too." Rogers asked, "What about the girls, Mabel and Bernice?" Coon said he "didn't see them- I shouted when I got there but everything was quiet." Coons went immediately to Stanfordville to report to his boss as the others sped to the Germond farm.

They found Mabel inside the kitchen door, her head in a pool of blood under the stove, (disproven by the facts) Bernice, on the far side of the room, was wedged between the legs of the sink and table. (See Exhibit# 21) They two had been stabbed five times each. Bernice's watch was stopped at 6:40 P.M. (Very limited value as evidence). Germond and Rogers hurried to the nearest telephone, which was in the house of a neighboring chicken farmer, Arthur J. Curry. With the help of the Curry's, the sheriff, doctors and neighbors were finally notified.

An army of investigators, professional and amateur, started to arrive at the crime scene. (See Exhibit #26) First to arrive were Undersheriff C. Fred Close and Deputy Martin R. Hicks. They notified the New York State police at Fishkill, 40 miles away. By early afternoon, village and county officials were vying with state police and newspapermen – to learn what had happened. (See Exhibit#26)

There was circumstantial evidence that Germond had been attacked first (the evidence refutes this claim). Near his body in the yard between the kitchen and the wagon shed, investigators found his pipe, screwdriver and his cap. He was stabbed four times. Apparently, his slayer dragged him feet first across the yard to the wagon shed. The dead man was still wearing his gold rimmed glasses. The pocket in which he carried his wallet was inside out (Sometimes used as a staging technique).. The wallet, which must have held less than $100, was gone. (The evidence showed the wallet would have contained far less than $100).

Burrs on the legs of Raymond's overalls indicated that he had fled into the field to escape. He was stabbed seven times and hauled back. (This is a very questionable account of the facts).

It was simple to assume that Mrs. Germond was set upon when she opened the back door and that the force of the attack caused her to spin about and fall, hitting her head on the stove. (Inaccurate account based on the scientific facts) Apparently, the slayer slashed out at her as she fell as her left leg was gashed by the knife (The cause of this injury became obvious) drops of blood fell on the doorstep. There was a small puddle inside the door and a large pool under the stove. (Very misleading description of the evidence) (See Exhibit #19) This is a rather pedestrian analysis of the blood that I will explore in detail later since it really is the best scientific evidence available at this late date. Bernice must have been reading at the table when she leaped up, to ward off the attacker (the evidence suggests otherwise). Her body, like her mother's body, lay undisturbed where it fell. The subsequent investigation demonstrated that a large amount of the foreign and even domestic media is shown to be mistaken in their analysis including even the domestic media and self-described reporters and personal investigators not to leave out magazine and book authors. The reader will note in a discovered crime scene photo contained herein as an exhibit that refutes unquestionably this perspective. (See Exhibit #'s 13, 21, 22)

A pair of brown cotton gloves, knife slashed and bloodstained, were on the table. Note, there are extensive forensic comments to follow later on with respect to these gloves. (See Exhibit #14)

Since Husted was a mild fellow with no known enemies and people of the farming community were not given to violent crimes, suspicion fell upon a gang of Spanish laborers who were working on highways out of Stanfordville, and living in a shack community about a mile from the Germond farm.

However, it turned out that all the workmen were present and accounted for between 5:20 and 6:40 Thanksgiving Eve at the time the murders must have been committed. (Note: the evidence indicates that three of the murders occurred before 5:20 P.M.) This scenario is part of the endless rumor mill discussed earlier.

Gossip spread a theory that the Husted Germond's were victims of mistaken identity. The story was that the Paul Germond family was marked for murder because Paul had driven scores of poachers- some of them highway construction workers – from his farm.

Paul thought this was far-fetched. The evidence agrees with his analysis as this was hardly a premeditated crime. The historical typologies in forensic science clearly agree with Paul's analysis. Endless evidence will be produced later in this volume to discount any notion of premeditation.

"The only motive I can think of," Paul said, "is robbery. But that doesn't seem likely when you think that Husted had only about $100 on him (much less) and whoever took that money didn't bother to take his good watch or his silver change. Y' know, Husted wasn't a man of means. I don't think his whole estate amounts to more than $5000 and most of that goes to mother. There's no friction or anything like that among our kin," he assured investigators, "Everyone's on friendly terms with all the others."

The Germond's Canadian-born neighbor Curry, who was a barber and roadhouse operator as well as a poultry farmer, suggested that the murderer might be someone who was jealous over young Bernice.

"When I cut her hair a few days ago," said Curry, "she told me she had a boyfriend she hoped to land over at that business school."

School authorities, on the other hand, told Assistant District Attorney Ely L. Gellert that Bernice was bashful, modest, retiring and had shown no romantic interest in any of the male students. The romantic relationships of Bernice Germond are regularly posited as the cause of this crime. Mr. Curry spent hours spreading this rumor as well as a District Attorney – even to this day this rumor continues. There is overwhelming evidence to refute this claim discussed at length later including perjury.

THE GERMOND FAMILY MURDERS

Three days after the bodies were found; several New York newspapermen hired William (Whitey) Leczyck, a Poughkeepsie cab driver, to take them to the Germond farm. Whitey was following the reporters about when one of his boots struck a butcher knife with an 11-inch blade. It was about 75 feet from the kitchen door on the far side of the fence. This it was later proven was the murder weapon, evidently tossed away by the killer after he had wiped it clean of prints.

The knife was traced to the Dubois Supply Co. in Poughkeepsie, where eleven such knives had been sold. Ten were traced to their owners. But on the eleventh, there was no record of sale (very strange number of sold knives in doubt).

One week after the murder, Germond's wallet was found in a culvert ½ mile from the Germond farm towards Paul's. His money was missing but his papers were intact.

It was recalled that a rough looking man got on the bus Bernice boarded in Poughkeepsie on her last trip home from school. The man asked for Bangall, two miles beyond the Germond place, but he alighted at Willow Brook, one-mile short of the Germond farm.

Now later that night this same stranger – or a man who looked like him – was seen walking along the highway from the direction of Stanfordville. He would certainly have passed by the spot where the wallet was found.

Still later, this rough looking man entered a store at Clinton Corners, a few miles from Stanfordville It must be pointed out here that there is absolutely no evidence on the surviving record that these appearances were of one and the same man, in fact, there is overwhelming evidence that it was not one and the same man. Speaking with an accent, he asked about buses to Poughkeepsie and was dissatisfied with the schedule given him by the storekeeper Oakley Robinson. He said he had to get to Poughkeepsie to get a train to Hudson because he had received a telegram that his mother was dying there. In that case, said Robinson, he thought transportation could be arranged.

While Robinson made a few telephone calls, the stranger drank two bottles of soda nervously and paid his 10-cent check with a dollar bill.

Then he bought a $1.50 wristwatch and paid for it with a $10 bill which had a stain on it. This stain is of absolutely no forensic value since the bills were inside Germond's wallet and one must ask why is it that a bill is stained, and the man is nicely dressed. If he had just stabbed four victims 23 times, he would be covered with blood – head to foot.

Finally, he agreed to pay $5 to Edward H. Wing and Floyd Younghans, two of Robinson's friends, to drive him to the Poughkeepsie railroad station. "He said he worked for Borden's and he gave a name like Florentine Chase," said Wing later. "He said he knew Ernie Nardone (a local sandbank operator) and Mike Saccomandi (a boarding house keeper). But he acted so funny I kept a tight grip on the crank handle all the way to Poughkeepsie just in case he got rough." (NOTE: comments to follow on these rather strange observations)

Borden's denied they had an employee named Florentine Chase or anything similar. None of the telegraph offices in the surrounding area had any record of transmitting or receiving word of a woman dying in Hudson. Nobody in Hudson knew anything about it either.

Nardone said he didn't know anybody named Florentine Chase. The only fellow he knew with that Christian name was Florentine Aispuri Firmendi, alias Bosco, who worked for a while on the highway construction job near the Germond farm.

This seemed like a hot lead and on December 13 Bosco was snatched out of a Brooklyn poolroom and brought to Dutchess County. There he was viewed by witnesses, but nobody could identify him as the rough looking stranger seen on the bus, the man later sighted on the road or the traveler in Robinson's store. Subjected to a stiff examination by District Attorney John R. Schwartz, Bosco denied that he was the Germond killer. He was held for 55 days as a material witness, then paid $110 ($2 per day) and released

Meanwhile, people were saying that there had been disagreements between Husted Germond and his neighbor, Curry, a small, slender, bespectacled fellow who kept his own counsel after he suggested that the Germond slayer might be found among Bernice's admirers.

THE GERMOND FAMILY MURDERS

The reader should keep in mind that the case was reopened in 1933 as will be discussed extensively later when all the evidence is discovered and the full forensic analysis is complete.

The gossip reached Sheriff Cookingham's ears (after the case was Reopened – see later analysis) and he employed the Pinkerton Detective Agency to consider it. Thus Capt. Daniel W. Fox, a Pinkerton man, came to Dutchess County.

Because of his investigation, Fox informed the Sheriff that Curry left his farm at 4 P. M. the day of the murders telling his wife he was going to the Germond's to collect a $30 annual rental on pasture land Germond was using. (There is a case of perjury here discussed later) Curry did not get home until 6:40 P.M. (NOTE: timing here is a major problem).

Two days later when everybody was talking about the Germond case. Curry told his wife; the killer must have reached the Germond farm right after he left it. He said he saw Germond but collected no money "and now we'll probably have to wait until after the Germond estate is settled."

On February 15, 1933, Cookingham had Mr. and Mrs. Curry and daughter, Betty, 9, brought to the office for questioning. They were released after lengthy interrogation, but three days later Curry was arrested as a material witness.

On March 8, Arthur Nemes (one of numerous suspects in the case easily disqualified later on) confessed that his second confession naming Steve Leko was false. And the next day, on Sheriff Cookingham's information, Curry was formally charged with the slaughter of the Germond family. The Sheriff's information was supported by several affidavits – but none provided direct evidence to link Curry with the killings. Confused yet? Stay tuned.

"Seldom has such a mild looking man (with a provable violent temper and a prison sentence at Sing Sing for assault) been accused of such horrible deeds," said one local commentator. Curry, 56, had a mustache and wore his hair parted in the center. He stood 5'10 and he weighed but 125 pounds. Please keep in mind that the forensic scientist is rarely interested in reputation so that the foregoing information is listed only because it is in the formal record.

Curry and his lawyer, Paul Rosen, appeared before Supreme Court Justice William F. Bleakley for a hearing on a writ of habeas corpus on April 3, 1933. After Sheriff Cookingham detailed his circumstantial evidence against Curry, the justice asked, "Did you form any opinion as to motive?"

"Well, Curry wanted Germond's pasture land for hunting privileges and I think they quarreled because Germond refused to let Curry post the land. Our investigation shows that the murders were the acts of a quick-tempered man after an argument."

In cross-examination by Rosen, the Sheriff denied that Curry was questioned for 56 hours in one stretch. He said that seven to eight hours was the longest period of interrogation. He did admit, however, that a detective, posing as a criminal wanted in the south for killing a revenue officer, was planted in Curry's cell in the hope of getting information from the suspect. The operative learned nothing.

When questioned about Curry's possible motive, Fox, the Pinkerton man, replied, "Curry needed the property and was sore because he could not get it back from under lease to Germond."

Then came the Poughkeepsie hardware dealer whose store was the source of the murder weapon. He was positive that he hadn't sold the knife to any member of the Curry family. All day long Justice Bleakley listened to testimony then he chastised Sheriff Cookingham.

"This case," he scolded "is lacking not only motive but proof. There are none of the attendant circumstances that usually occur in this type of crime. There are no admissions on the part of the defendant. Even if there were a confession, there is nothing to corroborate it. A lot of men would not be safe if we could go on evidence such as this."

Curry was freed and sued Sheriff Cookingham, but that case was dismissed. There is also the story of the stained bill accidently spent in Manhattan by an investigator. After Curry was freed, the case swung back to this mysterious man who has appeared in three places. As the totality of the evidence will demonstrate that this is a famous canard.

The behavior of Bernice Germond was widely viewed as the main basis in the formulation of a motive for this horrific crime. Mr. Curry made it a virtual mission of spreading rumors about Bernice for two years after the crime and his seemingly relentless pursuit of this *causa mortis* was adopted by many people including politicians, some law enforcement and prosecutors. Even the District Attorney was adamant about this until the day of his death,

District Attorney Schwartz opined:

"From various things I have heard, I am convinced that the explanation for the mystery is in the girl's life. I am led to believe that she went around with young men, unknown to her parents, and I think if we could reconstruct the history of her life, we might get a solution to this crime."

District attorney Schwartz made a career out of announcing the motive for the crime until the day he died. I do have a reason for this persistent behavior but it is not important to the facts in this case. It is contained in my analysis of Bernice's autopsy report about which I have chosen not to comment about for it lacks any scientific connection to this case and may appeal to some unstudied prurient interests. Actually, in the final report of this investigation, as will be shown later, Bernice's background was very carefully investigated and sworn testimony in the inquest minutes by numerous witnesses clearly demonstrates her lack of romantic activity.

This is a general narrative of the events. The final complete investigation would prove many of the foregoing events and the following media accounts to be totally disproven. One would be surprised to find that even current older residents of the area still endorse these motives and rumors. Careful what you read in the papers and in books.

There were three or four notable suspects in this case that will be extensively examined and exonerated as the victims of rumor and reputation I will demonstrate the lack of plausibility in each case.

Let's take a look next.

CHAPTER 3

The Media and Rumors

IN ORDER TO demonstrate the absurdity of some media accounts on this case, I take the reader to the New York Daily News, December 9, 1930, page 35. Therein you will find a report that the reporter is informed by those at the scene that an unidentified "Horseman" was believed to be the offender as hooves prints have been found in the ground near the murder scene. Apparently, some macabre jokester told a reporter this preposterous story at the scene and the reporter not only "bought it hook line and sinker" but actually printed it. As if that wasn't bad enough, the same report claimed that the murder scene was actually 17 miles away from Stanfordville and that the crime occurred in the kitchen. I was not able to locate a retraction of this utterly bizarre story anywhere in the record. It was the wildest of all rumors and reports and I just couldn't resist telling it first.

It might be helpful to now review some of the contemporary media coverage to provide a general background for those not familiar with the case. In addition, conflicting information will be discussed as well as the endless theories and rumors. The included comments will indicate issues disproven by the eventual scientific evidence. One of the important results in obtaining all the actual records of a particular case is the ability to disprove the media reports and "accepted" rumors that developed over the years. Even more shocking, are the authors and publishers who have now the opportunity to publish all

THE GERMOND FAMILY MURDERS

the facts and correct that which they have written over the years but have refused to do so. There are even authors who continue to write articles about this rather famous case, who have been made aware of the facts, continue to write what now must be regarded as utter nonsense given the scientific evidence.

I have personally contacted numerous authors, publishers, magazine editors and individuals concerning the facts of this case. I have provided each and every one with the scientific facts that I have uncovered as a result of the court ordered investigation without a single reply or desire to correct the record. Not one party could provide any substantive further evidence worthy of continued investigation of any probative value

The following are a mere sample of some of the publications where contemporary "facts" are now shown to be scientifically inaccurate.

Poughkeepsie Newspaper, "The Eagle News," on Saturday, November 30, 1930 by Charles Murray, got right into the story by merely asking random citizens. Shortly after the bodies of the Germond family were discovered, a "Mysterious stranger," subsequently identified by his own words as "Florentine Chase," appeared several times or at least a similar man in appearance. Chase was placed on the roads near the farm near the time of the slayings. He was described as a "foreigner." He entered the store at Clinton Corners (the town adjacent to Stanfordville). He told the proprietor, Oakleigh Robinson, that he was an employee of the Borden Creamery in Stanfordville. He claimed his mother was seriously ill in Hudson and he wanted to go there. He spoke poor English and continued to inquire how he might get to Poughkeepsie. It was now 8:00 P.M. the night of the murders. The witness stated that he "paced nervously in and out of the store, apparently in great mental distress." Mr. Robinson contacted Edward Wing to drive "Chase" to the railroad station in Poughkeepsie for $5.00. Wing, for reasons unknown was suspicious of Chase and contacted the Borden Creamery who advised him that they had no such employee as Florentine Chase. Wing then recruited Floyd Younghands to accompany him. Mr. Younghands claimed that he became nervous

THE MEDIA AND RUMORS

in the car on the way to Poughkeepsie so much so that he grabbed the crank handle and tightly held it fearful of an attack. If this same man was the offender, where was he for the past two- and one-half hours since the provable completion of the crime?

We must also keep in mind that none of the persons who encountered Chase or the "mysterious stranger" was aware that any crime had been committed. However, their responses were documented after the crimes were well known and that Florentine Chase matched the description of the "Mysterious stranger." It should be noted that descriptions do vary. However, Chase was described as well dressed. The perpetrator of this crime would be literally drenched in blood spatter even of moderate intensity like a gunshot wound assuming that I understand the injuries correctly at this point in my inquiry. However, the subsequent analysis of autopsy reports validated my interpretation. In addition, it has been my experience having investigated hundreds of serious crimes that some witnesses will welcome their Andy Warhol fifteen minutes of fame and seem to internalize their witness statements and even confirm (unconsciously) the statements of others. For example, Mr. Younghands claimed that during the ride to Poughkeepsie, he "kept a tight grip on the crank handle." Mr. Younghands had absolutely no knowledge that any crime was committed at all. He was, as do many witnesses, channeling Andy Warhol. The reporters should have been very suspicious of claims by people who couldn't possibly have been aware of the crime. So, the story continued.

Some investigators believed the house was made to look like a robbery scene, drawers open, etc. In addition, $100 was missing from James Germond's pocket. Police did not believe the robbery theory for some unknown reason. Police believed that a man acquainted with the daughter (Bernice) who was, most likely "repulsed" by her. A theory consistently peddled by Mr. Curry. They were persuaded that there was a good reason for that speculation. Two years earlier, "a Spaniard insulted" Bernice and was fired when Mr. Germond complained. This "laborer" they contend threatened "to get" them and kill them all to prevent them from identifying him.

This is all very interesting speculation. Two points come to mind. First, I agree that a crime of rage is more likely than simple robbery and the staging of crime scenes is usually very sloppy. Secondly, robbery can be in tandem with a crime of rage indicating that the offender knew that Mr. Germond just received some cash giving rise to the "local laborer" theory. The problem with Bernice being the target, is lessened by the evidence when the bus driver heard her remark that the "house was dark" when it should have lamps on given the Thanksgiving preparations that were underway. If this is accurate then Bernice surprised the intruder as she was found on the other side of the room where her mother was lying and there is no evidence that she was killed in defense of her mother. Moreover, there is evidence to the contrary – there is witness evidence that Bernice's hat and coat were hanging in the hallway by the front door – further proof that she entered from the front door. The same article continued two days later by repeating rumors and theories. Steve Leko lived on a farm near Stanfordville and investigators believed he "fit a description." A Dr. Richardson claimed he saw Leko walking on the road near the Germond farm at the time of the murders. He "lied repeatedly to investigators." However, Dr. Richardson later stated that he made a mistake and that he saw Leko on Thanksgiving morning. Leko admitted that he was there at that time. (More about Leko later).

If Leko was involved in this crime or anyone else for that matter, they would have been covered with both blood spatter and even indirect or arterial expulsion. The whole record does not indicate the seizure of clothes or any application for a search warrant to search for any. Forensic serological capabilities were limited in those days, but some did exist including presumptive tests. I will discuss these technical issues later.

Poughkeepsie Eagle News, Wednesday, December 3, 1930 continues.Lt. Thomas Whalen was the owner of the farm leased to the Germond family. He boarded up the buildings sometime after the crime arguing that "none will rent it now." He was wrong. Family

THE MEDIA AND RUMORS

memorials were held in near zero weather and Sheriff Rockefeller remained at the door of the services with Mr. Byron Hicks who was the salesman of the alleged murder weapon (knife) of the Dubois Supply Co. It was hoped that Hicks could identify the person to whom he sold the knife. Mr. Hicks testimony was indeed unusual and questionable. The numerous local papers continued obviously due to the fame of the crime. Herman Soloway, a City of Poughkeepsie Police Detective, was called in to assist with the case. He observed that "the scene was destroyed" and too many police and bystanders were on the scene. He noticed that there were very few experienced detectives with homicide experience. He quit. No media inquiries. This is a frequent problem in police work with competing jurisdictions and the "Military Management Model" in law enforcement. Too many chiefs not enough Indians – lots of chiefs running through the scene pretending to know what they are looking at – unchallenged and giving unstudied orders. It was particularly egregious in this case and may have contributed to a failure to solve the case. Many dozens of onlookers repeatedly trod through the entire crime scene. In fact, as will be discussed later, most of the physical evidence was found by non-law enforcement personnel. There was a seemingly endless army of citizen detectives.

A media account here claimed that an investigator accidentally spent a blood stained $10 bill "doing police legwork in NYC" (a very charitable description indeed). Others claimed it was only a $1 bill. Blood can assume many colors on different surfaces. I view this story as lacking any probative value. With respect to the stained bill, there is some persuasive evidence that it was a $1 bill and not a $10. In addition, the "stain" on the bill could have been from any other form of trace evidence.

I don't want this commentary to seem like I'm picking on the Poughkeepsie Journal but this newspaper was the local paper at the time and for many years after they printed endless stories and speculation about this case. A large volume of their reporting has been shown to be scientifically inaccurate. However, I have contacted the paper

THE GERMOND FAMILY MURDERS

many times to correct the record including the editor and publisher personally with registered mail. No person from the Poughkeepsie Journal has ever responded to any communication that I have sent to them including endless phone calls.

The New York Times really gets involved here. They Offered a $25 thousand reward for information. In the interest of truth in broadcasting and writing, I am no fan of the New York Times having read their reports of incidents where I was actually present and didn't really recognize some of the events. Even after three years on this case, they still couldn't get it right. On March 18, 1933, when the case was reopened. They reported that a person was "Held in Slaying of Four Germonds." The problem was that they got some of the facts wrong. They got the location wrong and misstated who found some of the bodies and his behavior thereafter. They incorrectly reported the person who called the police. Ten days after the crime the New York Times, December 7, 1930 reported that on December 6, James Germond's "pocketbook" was found with no money but with his driver's licenses, some cards and papers. It was found in a "culvert" on Willow Brook about ½ mile south of the Germond farm in the direction of the farm of James's brother Paul Germond. In this case the Times lurched uncontrollably into the partial truth. It was actually and obviously a men's wallet and was found on the road next to a culvert in the direction of Willow Brook. It was not near Paul Germond's farm This event is another crucial reason for the careful development of a crime scene sketch. None have been located or even commented on by prior "investigators." I have prepared some rough crime scene sketches myself. (See Exhibits #'s 2 & 2A) The discovery, of the wallet, was thought to suggest that the mysterious man at Robinson's store in Clinton Corners must have been the murderer since the wallet was found in the direction of Clinton Corners. However, other adjoining properties were nearby as well. Hence, the value of an accurate crime scene sketch. The New York Times, December 15, 1930 said that Florentino Aispuru Eirmendi, 27 was a highway laborer and was identified as the man who hired a car to drive him to a bus stop on

THE MEDIA AND RUMORS

Thanksgiving Eve. This account is provably false on the sworn record. This occurred at Clinton Corners, three miles from the murder scene. Florentino was actually arrested at 90 Baltic Street, Brooklyn, New York. He had "blood stains" on his jacket but claimed they were from wine. He produced an alibi with witnesses who said he was at home. This report was even disproven a couple of years after the crime yet has survived to this day as gospel. I was always eager to find the report of this matter but no such report was ever located in the surviving documents It is hard to believe as reported.

Also, the various sighting of different strangers in the case cannot be taken seriously. There is absolutely no evidence that they were all one and the same. The more important question is: why would a man who had just committed a horrible crime and who must have been covered with blood from head to foot, wander around the roads of Stanfordville simply inviting apprehension? In addition, this man probably had "cuts" on his own hand from his use of a very slippery knife having been thrust into four human beings for a total of 23 times. I have just listed a few of these inaccuracies here as I could have listed many dozens more.

However, I'd like to provide two final examples. In 2019, Modern Farmer wrote a major article about this case, I read it and found endless errors of fact. I contacted Modern Farmer and spoke to several of its publishers offering them the opportunity to print a correction of the story and promised to send them the facts, they refused and showed no interest in the matter. In addition, a book was written by Andrew K. Amelinckx, "Hudson Valley, Murder & Mayhem," contains many proven errors of fact discovered in the investigation from the Court Order. I contacted Mr. Amelinckx on several occasions and discussed with him the errors in his work and suggested that he write a follow-up. No such follow-up was ever forthcoming as of this writing. Moreover, I discussed the article that he wrote in "Modern Farmer" on October 31, 2007 also containing similar errors. Just like my response from discussions with Modern Farmer publishers, no such correction or follow-up has been published.

It should be noted that Mr. Amelinckx was quite convivial in our conversations and seemed interested in my findings. Moreover, he stated that he would collaborate with Modern Farmer to do a follow-up. He is obviously a talented writer and man of professional deportment. Accordingly, I am quite surprised that neither he nor Modern Farmer have taken any steps in furtherance of a follow-up.

The Rumor Mill Continues

In my three full years of work, I was able to locate at least ten highly publicized rumors that gained widespread support and attention including some writers and newspapers that seemingly endorsed some of them. Most of these rumors were easily disproven by the discovered evidence as well as contradictory statements. Other rumors must be regarded as the manifestations of imaginative minds, still a few were patently preposterous.

I could not devote the time to all the rumors gathered over the years concerning this crime. I cite a few here as a demonstration as to the types of disprovable scenarios that have been promoted. There was a report by an area resident that a local person was hiding under the bridge over Wappinger's Creek and overheard the whole crime and claimed that Husted Germond's brother Paul was the offender. This person claimed to have been able to see and hear the entire crime as it unfolded. In response to this claim, I conducted several experiments (discussed later) at the actual scene and spent several days thereat evaluating this claim. High intensity magnification and sound devices were used. In addition, the conditions at the time of the crime were well known and taken seriously into consideration. The bridge in question stands today exactly as it did at the time of the crime and the dimensions are exact but foliage is entirely different as photographic evidence indicated. The bridge is slightly north of the Germond home and approximately 295 feet away. The wagon shed is another 155 feet further. Wappinger's Creek is a rapidly moving stream at this time of the year at this point and makes a distinct sound of rushing water. The witness would have had to climb down the bank and conceal himself from view further obstructing both vision and sound. I was unable to hear a conversation from even the roadway in front of the house. The sound of the stream from this point made any noises unintelligible. (See Exhibit #6). In addition, Paul Germond had an iron-clad alibi – eyewitnesses put him at his farm at the approximate time of the crime. He would have needed helicopter assistance to have been a reasonable suspect in order to travel from his farm to and from the crime scene. In addition, his father-in-law would have to have been a co-conspirator because he was with Paul Germond during this event by sworn statements. A further claim was made indicating that the Willow Brook was the location of the interloper. The Willow Brook is in fact closer to the Germond house but different issues exist. There would be no advantageous point to conceal oneself at this location as concealment at the time and absent any foliage would have easily caused the discovery of the observer particularly since some of the crime was committed outside of the house in the open yard next to Willow Brook. In short, this claim lacks any form of reasonable probative value.

There was a rumor that the Germond family was killed by mistake and that Paul Germond was the real target. As a change of pace, the Germonds were killed by bootleggers and organized crime because the Germonds were alleged to be government informants about illicit stills in the area. This claim was carefully evaluated and dismissed for three major reasons:

1. This is absolutely not the typology of murder utilized by revenge assassins or organized crime then or even now,
2. Anyone who knew the Germond family well, made no such claim and even dismissed this speculation as "ridiculous,"
3. Nowhere in the official record is there contained any serious investigation involving this claim nor is there any noted involvement of any federal authority or collateral investigation.

I came upon a site on "Reddit" written by a surviving relative of the Germond family who has apparently conducted a superficial search of the crime. It was a reasonable account but contained some material misstatements of fact. However, the hundreds of comments that followed contained endless errors of fact, science and logic.

Another famous rumor reported endlessly in commentaries and media is that the Germond case is still an "open case." This is false. The case was officially closed in 1960 with re-interviews. I am actually in possession of the New York State Police closing investigative report though FOIA discovery. Many researchers continue to claim that Florentine Chase purchased the murder weapon. This is provably false. Extensive evidence on the record not only disproves this claim but it should be remembered that no such person as "Florentine Chase" was ever identified. He was in fact a made-up name by the man in the store in Clinton Corners.

This type of investigative work took a great deal of my time away from the actual evidence but it had to be done. Many of these theories and rumors exist to this day and there are even contemporary writers who comment on them as though they have never been disproven. Some readers might even find it interesting to explore the totality of the theories and rumors that I uncovered in this case. To record them all, would require another volume. However, such was not my task under the court order but invariably had to be investigated.

CHAPTER 4

Further Initial Case Observations

Introduction to a Cold Case

A very brief introduction to the routine practices of A FORENSIC SCIENTIST regarding rumors, speculation, reputation, group think and first impressions as well as the science and typologies etc. seems now appropriate.

When examining cold cases, the investigator must avoid several unhelpful pitfalls. First, he must not seem to be a "know it all" whereby he creates an ease in the case not present for the contemporary investigators. In short, he must avoid socio-historical guilt systems. Secondly, he must come to understand the inherent unfairness of examining a case eighty-eight years ago with current resources and technology. Finally, there must be a recognition that criticizing the police is an American art form. Everybody knows more than the cops, after all, if they were so smart, they'd be lawyers. Lawyers all perceive themselves as social critics and they consider themselves investigators after the fact. Few are mindful of the great aphorism: "These are the saddest words of song and pen: stories of what might have been."

In accepting the Germond Family Murders for cold case analysis, I based my views on years of experience in many capacities relevant to forensic and crime-scene investigation. Moreover, if one might perceive that I am a critic of this case, keep in mind that the investigating officer, appointed in 1933, Sheriff Oakleigh Cookingham, was a

THE GERMOND FAMILY MURDERS

relative as I am told – a total coincidence.

A systematic review of all the retained physical and documentary evidence preserved at the Dutchess County Sheriff's Office in Poughkeepsie, New York was undertaken as well as the resources of involved agencies. Numerous visits to the actual crime scene were conducted to gain a more accurate dimensional perspective.

It is obvious from the initial interviews that the total case file has not been fully retained and most of the physical evidence has long since been removed. The photographic evidence that has been retained is quite helpful. In fact, several photos enabled me to draw some very specific scientific conclusions.

At the end, I have made my best inference as to the probable killer or his / her prototype. I will draw this inference not for its current probative value, but in what direction the retained fact pattern leads us. In addition, I will identify the contemporary forensic techniques available at the time of the crime and how the economy of forensic scholarship has led us to the present. Where truly serious mishandling can be observed, it was noted without prejudice. The real bottom line is that I must have access to all the files in this case that are being held by the Medical Examiner, District Attorney and the Chief Clerk's archives. A court order is the only avenue to obtain these documents since the only real evidence for which I have initial access are the crime scene photos. Not to be downplayed, these photos, when properly analyzed, have substantive probative value in forming a more definitive final opinion in this case. The photos are widely available on the public record in books and magazines as well as public exhibits of the photos by the Dutchess County Sherriff's Office. In addition, I was personally informed by the Records Officer that many prior investigators have seen them and retained copies of them. Moreover, all the files for which I have litigated and opined have not been published nor will they be published as per the order of the court (see Exhibit #'s 30, 30A and 31).

FURTHER INITIAL CASE OBSERVATIONS

The Available Preserved Evidence – First Examination

The current available evidence (initial examination) is extremely scant. No crime scene sketches are available, no autopsy reports are available (yet) and the contents of some interviews are indeed inadequate though absolutely none of them contained in the Sheriff's Office are published or will be published herein or elsewhere. In short "there isn't much left." However, I'll try. The current crime scene is private property and basically hidden from certain compass readings and line of site laser measurements. However, the actual crime scene in 1930 was rather open and with very limited vegetation. Further, sketching as well as recently discovered claims of a deceased witness are reviewed. If you think that you've seen complicated cases, wait until you read about this one 90 years after it happened. The initial crime scene was never secured and a proper search for evidence was never accomplished. I realize that the contemporary law enforcement personnel had very limited experience in such matters, but very basic steps were never taken. Even the "Jack the Ripper" case in 1880's London, police secured each crime scene and conducted an orderly search for evidence.

Many documented interviews were filled with reputational information and totally bereft of any forensic analysis or probative evidentiary value. The preserved documented record is bereft of any skilled analysis and, at times, difficult to read with typos and syntax problems not to mention misspellings. As a matter of fact, there were absolutely no documentation of any probative value obtained at the Sheriffs Office other then the crime scene photos which had been widely distributed over the decades. People and investigators started connecting all weird people and circumstances to the Germond case. Most of this is contained in the 1933 report during Sheriff Cookingham's involvement in the case reproduced in very poorly written summary form by a contemporary staff member. More is also found in "Synopsis - Germond Murder." Though subject to appropriate criticism, Sherriff Cookingham's documentation is somewhat better though lacking in forensic value and probative evidence. In short, the professional forensic science community would consider this report of marginal value and lacking in skilled preparation. In short, no documents located at the Sheriff Office have been used in this case or reproduced.

It should be noted that the existing investigative file is very limited in scope and much has been lost over the last 88 years. The current staff at the Dutchess County Sheriff's Office deserves a great deal of credit for preserving what remains. It seems to have been "picked over" during the passage of years and much is missing especially autopsy reports, crime scene sketches, more enhanced forensic photography, affidavits, et al. Also missing are the personal effects of the victims and their clothing. Even at this late date, some current forensic applications could still be applied to this evidence. This was not an easy cold case to review. In fact, I was about to "through in the towel" when I first reviewed what was left. In fairness, the investigators at the time were not experienced people. In fact, there is very persuasive evidence on the record that no real efforts were made to preserve the crime scene. The day of the discovery of the crime, many dozens of people had wandered about the house and within days, literally hundreds of people had been on the scene. A memorial service was held at the crime scene for the family within days and many hundreds of people were present. (See Exhibit #26)

The narrative to follow is taken primarily from public and media records NOT the evidence. However, I will opine strictly on the evidence and inferences drawn from intelligence guided by experience. Some of the reports are proven to be accurate and others demonstrably false. I have listed a large sample of the public record earlier. It is but a small sample as this case was reported nationwide and at least two European dailies. I am going to use the most accurate that I found in the New York Daily News, "Justice Story," Sunday, December 1, 1957, p.118 ff. by Ruth Reynolds. Original copies of this work are extremely rare. Your humble investigator retains one of the originals. This was a 25-year attempt to revive interest in the case. This article got "most" of the basic story accurately. My summary of the public record follows:

FURTHER INITIAL CASE OBSERVATIONS

History and Background of the Case
November 26, 1930

In 1930, Stanfordville, New York was a dairy farming community about 100 miles north of New York City inhabited by many German immigrants who were farmers by trade. This is not to say that many other ethnic cohorts were not residing and farming there as well. Your humble investigator is related to many of them. This was an entirely trusting community where people depended closely on one another. Diligent attempts have been made to explore the following information and make my best approximation as to the facts and circumstances, in fact, they are crucial steps in such an investigation.

- Approximate time of occurrence
- Order of the homicides
- Recovered Evidence
- Crime scene evaluation
- Suspects
- Crime scene sketch
- Order of potential flight
- Best evidence
- Contemporary police handling of the crime scene and evidence
- Forensic techniques that was available at the time.
- Autopsy Evidence

In 1933, after extensive public pressure, then Governor Franklin Roosevelt not only reopened the case, but claimed a solution was at hand. Roosevelt, in his successful bid for the presidency, failed to carry his home Dutchess County. Anyway, when President-elect Roosevelt returned in December to Hyde Park which isn't far from the Germond farm – he said that the Germond mystery had been solved.

This proved that Roosevelt was much better as a politician than as a detective. For his statement was predicated on a new "confession" by young Nemes in which the boy said his "recantation had been incorrect." However, nobody bothered Leko and the Germond mystery passed its second anniversary. I have investigated the claims of Messer's Leko and Nemes extensively and have also concluded that the stories involving these two witnesses are not only lacking in credibility but are contradicted by forensic science evidence.

Having reviewed all the available evidence located in the (limited) files of the Dutchess County Sheriff's Office, several obvious leads stood out to me that may have contained the solution to this case. It was hard for me to fathom that these issues were not obvious to the initial investigators. However, the initial investigators were not experienced forensic investigators nor were the commentators to follow in the subsequent 90 years.

The solution to this case would revolve around several obvious issues that were apparent to me:

1. Timing,
2. Measurements,
3. Illumination,
4. Capacity,
5. Conflicting statements,
6. Crime Scene photos,
7. Evidence handling,
8. Witness statements,
9. Blood patterns.

When one reviews and analyses the 1144 pages of inquest minutes and 200 witnesses (mostly sworn) as I have, the issues described here become crucial and quite revealing.

Timing

All recovered evidence to this point demonstrated specific time coordination between the scene of the crime, location of suspects and the sworn statements of witnesses as well as suspects.

FURTHER INITIAL CASE OBSERVATIONS

Measurement

Distances had to be computed to match existing statements and reports to determine the probative value of reports on the record. Various technical tests were conducted using sensitive equipment described later.

Illumination - Visibility

Since most of the crime was committed in virtual darkness and the culmination of the crime was in fact committed in darkness, illumination testing and visibility had to be conducted. These technical forensic tests will be described later. There are numerous reasons why illumination and visibility are crucial to the solution to this case;

1. The arrival of the bus in front of the Curry residence on Rt. 82 as to whether or not numerous passengers could have seen about which they testified to and signed sworn affidavits,
2. Tests were conducted at the same time of day at the very locations of the bus and the testimony of the witness who remained in front of the residence for fifteen minutes awaiting pick-up by her father – her distance was 123 feet away – our tests confirmed all the witness testimony,
3. Tests of visibility (using measured historic headlight lumens) of the approaching bus at 5:20 P.M. approaching the Germond home on the Salt Point Turnpike – even with current vegetation and trees, the barn yard was easily visible with bus headlights at 355 feet. This is crucial since only one person could have known that the bus would stop in front of the house and the bodies would easily be visible. The headlights are observable for at least 3/8 mile away making escape and concealment of the bodies necessary. If one was not aware of the bus stopping then escape was easy from virtually all directions.

Lighting and visibility add great weight to a solution in this case since they limit the capacity of almost all suspects but one.

Pre-knowledge of this bus is crucial to a solution in this case eventually and explains certain conduct of the offender that only he could have acted upon.

Capacity

Since there existed numerous suspects identified on the preserved record and since there were endless rumors and media speculation, numerous tests of physical capacity had to be conducted. These tests will be described later. It was the previously described tests that were of the most probative value.

Conflicting statements

I have described here what many investigators call the "Andy Warhol Effect." Many witnesses to famous crimes actually perceive themselves in the middle of the crime as witnesses either actual or imagined. Some also will exaggerate their observations in order to feel more prominent in the case. Still others will endorse rumors as if they actually witnessed it. Most of these people are not bad people; they are merely channeling their Andy Warhol "Fifteen minutes of fame." Nonetheless, they must all be evaluated and weighted against more substantive evidence to issue them whatever credibility that the fact pattern merits.

Crime scene photos

There are approximately 22 usable crime scene photos that were enlarged by the initial investigators to aid them in their inquiry. Some of them are not only helpful, but form the very gravamen of the solution to this case. It is apparent that the initial investigators missed this evidence but very few were knowledgeable in Blood Pattern Analysis (BPA). I will provide a rather limited discussion of this scientific concept later.

FURTHER INITIAL CASE OBSERVATIONS

Evidence Handling

The extent and value of evidence handling is crucial to a multiple homicide case or any other major case for that matter. In this case, not only was the evidence not handled correctly; it wasn't handled at all. Most of the evidence was discovered by non-law enforcement personnel. In fact, the crime scene was never secured or preserved in any meaningful way. Photos after the crime show the scene to take on a virtual carnival atmosphere.

Witness Statements

There are no witness statements preserved in the record at the Sheriff's Office and they are of varying quality. Some notes display grammatical and spelling deficiencies and some others are utterly unintelligible. Some statements are taken under oath as is normal and others do not have the usual sworn component. However, we must assume that they were all understood to be under oath. However, all subsequent statements reviewed at the County Clerk's Office and the District Attorney's Office are seemingly under oath. These are reviewed and opined upon after the issuance of the Court Order,

This is probably a good point to review some of the actual scientific applications used in this case and they include the following:

1. Sound
2. Lighting
3. Measurements & Distance
4. Blood Evidence
5. Photo evidence enhancements
6. Timing
7. Fingerprinting

Sound

In the previous commentary on "rumors," I discussed a claim that a person was concealed near a bridge and overheard and saw some of the crime. The scene was inspected at length here extensively and routine tests were conducted. We were not able to hear even minimal conversations from these locations and unable to provide audio of any testing. However, it should be remembered that the current scene contains extensive vegetation whereas at the time of the crime, the point from the position at the bridge to the barnyard was free from vegetation. The open space would have aided in the audition but we found that the running stream neutralized this advantage. In addition, the view is somewhat obstructed by the turning of the road. We concluded that this claim lacked any probative value and based on the already known forensic evidence, the claim is inconsistent with the facts.

Lighting

Lighting is a very significant issue in the solution of this case. It becomes important in two particular instances. First, the arrival of the bus containing Bernice Germond at 5:20 P.M. Secondly, the view of the Curry residence from the other bus arriving on the County Road (now Rt. 82). The brightness of headlights can be measured in lumens. The average bus headlights in pre-1940 New York was found to be about 2000 lumens. Today, a bus can generate 3500 lumens easily. Tests were conducted on the Salt Point Turnpike approaching the Germond residence using both measurements. From approximately 200 feet away from the yard where the blood spot was seen in exhibit photos, 2000 lumens lit up that area very well even though there is foliage where it did not exist at the time of the crime. (See Exhibit #10) Any person on the bus at that time would have easily seen bodies lying in the yard so that their removal was imperative for one seeking to delay discovery and doubly important for one who knows that this bus will stop right in front of the Germond home. In the case of the bus passing by the Curry residence, that still stands to this day in the same environmental condition as at the time of this crime, the approaching bus would have stopped no more than 150 away from the front porch of this residence and would have allowed anyone on the bus to see a person standing thereon. (See Exhibit #5) In addition, tests demonstrated that bus lights would have illuminated the entire front of this residence from as far away as 400 feet until arrival at the front door. There are three sworn affidavits on the record from passengers who swore that no lights were on and that no person was standing on that porch for the times stated.

Measurements and Distance

Many measurements and distance data were conducted in this case in order to demonstrate both capacity, timing and access. There are many comments throughout my work that will refer to events and distances including the use of laser measurements as well as scientific distance modeling with the help of the office of the Dutchess County Clerk.

Blood Patterns

If there ever was one element that led me to a solution, it is the blood patterns clearly shown in crime scene photos. Later on, the official autopsies would confirm my analysis. No part of the recovered and discovered evidence in this case is more important than the blood patterns analyzed from the crime scene photos. In fact, the very solution to this case was largely dependent on the Blood Pattern Analysis (BPA). It should be remembered that my analysis is based on the enhancements of crime scene photos whereas on-scene analysis is the more definitive protocol. Perhaps this is a good point to begin a limited tutorial on Blood Pattern Analysis.

Forensic Scientists can determine a great deal by the blood discovered at a crime scene. Terms such as cast off, splatter, droplets, etc. can reveal where the blood came from and the direction of the force or even, as in this case, gravitational droplets from one being held and where there exists limited or definable blood trails. The crime scene photos, listed as exhibits at the end, will contain explanations as to which scientific term was used to gain information from these photos. In addition, numerous scientific formulas can be used to determine both distance and angle. For example, calculus can be used to determine the angle that exists in the blood striking the surface. Moreover, mathematical use can be applied in determine both Areas of Concentration and Areas of Origin (and area of convergence). In fact, this technique (among others) was used in this case to prove by approximation that there were two separate crimes in the kitchen of the Germond home. The exhibits at the end will be more carefully described to enhance understanding. Obviously, I had to make my best scientific approximations based on the crime scene photos since actual on scene measurements were never made and much of the forensic knowledge of blood pattern analysis was unknown to initial investigators.

Fingerprints

Perhaps a brief discussion of fingerprints seems appropriate since the recovered evidence discusses finger prints of both a suspect and the murder weapon. Fingerprints for our purposes here, may be said to include two types: latent and patent. Some like the term plastic. I conducted a comparison of patent prints on the murder weapon with known prints of a suspect. There were two photos of the knife. One with plastic prints visible and the other clear. I found no known reason for this since it was claimed on the record that the offender "wiped the knife clean of prints." I discus this analysis later. A latent print must be developed to be seen and compared whereas a patent print is visible usually because some substance was already on the fingers when applied to the tested surface.

It must be kept in mind that fingerprints prove ONLY contact and nothing else unattended with other evidence. There is no evidence on the recovered record of any elimination prints nor the recording of fingerprint evidence searches or comparisons. This is a distinct forensic failing even back in 1930.

For those amateur sleuths out there, if you want some more technical reading on Blood Pattern Analysis and / or fingerprinting as well as crime scene analysis, I recommend the work of Richard Saferstein, Ph.D. in *Forensic Science From the Crime Scene to the Crime Lab,* third edition, 2016. Dr. Saferstein is a leading figure in this field. Some of this material is rather technical but he explains it quite well with photos and exhibits.

FURTHER INITIAL CASE OBSERVATIONS

Since forensic science was in the preparadigmatic stage in 1930, that does not mean that some well-established principles were not being observed. For example, the Jack-The-Ripper case in the 1890's, contains preserved evidence even to this day. In fact, in 2001, blood analysis was conducted on a leather apron and some clothing that actually identified human blood but lacked a basis of comparison. It is a well-established principle (even then) to preserve potential evidence where there may develop techniques in the future that may form the basis of scientific analysis. A good example, would be the preservation of the gloves found at the crime scene. These gloves would almost certainly have contained blood specimens of both the victim and the offender. The weapon used was a type of kitchen cutlery that did not contain a knife guard. Accordingly, the force of the stab wounds would have caused the slices in the gloves as a result of slippage of the hand. When blood exits the human body, it is quite warm and exceedingly slippery like motor oil. Some objects were preserved but were absconded by makeshift detectives and others – they were never properly preserved and apparently this process never occurred to law enforcement at the time.

To be completely fair, it should be noted that there were no contemporary law enforcement personnel at the time of this crime who were experienced in major crime-scene investigation. However, there were personnel of the New York State Police and the Pinkerton Agency who were familiar with basic forensic strategies. Most particularly, crime scene protection, organized search, preservation of evidence and crime-scene sketching. In addition, investigators notes that included lighting, measurements, witness statements and environmental conditions were never located. So bad was the handling of this case that an experienced detective from the Poughkeepsie Police Department was recruited to help and he immediately excused himself from the scene based on what he initially observed, saying, "this place is a mess, you'll never solve it." The fact that I could not locate any investigator's notes is rather startling and unprofessional even then.

The continuous pilfering of the saved evidence over the years by amateur investigators is absolutely inexcusable. Most critically, the loss of the Husted Germond autopsy protocol would, in my judgement, be crucial to a solution to this case.

CHAPTER 5

Trying to get All the Evidence Must Reopen the Case

EVERY CRIMINAL INVESTIGATOR realizes that gathering evidence is extremely difficult at times. It is ever more difficult in cold cases. Therefore, I continued my search for more information through media but all I found was repetition of previous publications. So, I tried to find competent investigators over the years who have looked at this case and all I could find were writers acting as investigators instilling their work with self-developed theories of their own, that in most cases were easily defeated by the actual evidence. Some of the theories even called into question the seriousness of the writer given how utterly preposterous they were.

During my many trips to Stanfordville over several years looking for even people who were old who remembered some of the facts or even people who followed the case over the years since there would be regular articles every few years in the Poughkeepsie Journal repeating the same story containing the same inaccuracies. I made endless attempts to contact the Poughkeepsie Journal without success even sending registered mail to both the editor and publisher without response. I sent information and communications to even to officials of the Town of Stanford without a response. In one instance a town official hung up the phone on me. My efforts were totally not for profit and only historic at my own expense but few found that of interest. In the later stages of my investigation, I made several calls to the Dutchess County Sheriff seeking a meeting without any call back. However, later on I received a call from a staff member asking me what I wanted and I simply dismissed this as unhelpful. The Sheriff was never available.

I was able to make some very important contacts of highly professional individuals who played a very significant role in the solution of this case. They will be fully acknowledged throughout. I did meet with the County Historian, though a very affable fellow, didn't seem interested in this case or my work.

New Developments – Autopsy Reports

As a result of the highly professional assistance of Mr. Bradford Kendall, Dutchess County Clerk, the Germond autopsy reports were located and are preserved in County archives.

I began email communications with Mr. Kendall and County Attorney Christopher Cullen whereupon I was advised that a Court Order was necessary to view these reports. Mr. Kendall under the guidance of Mr. Cullen filed a petition before the New York State Supreme Court on my behalf seeking disclosure.

On February 15, 2018 the New York State Supreme Court denied my request stating that I must be the petitioner and not Mr. Kendall.

Mr. Kendall then sought alternative legal strategies.

Case Takes A Major Turn

Mr. Kendall's enthusiasm came up big as he introduced me to Judge Rosenblatt of the Poughkeepsie law firm of McCabe & Mack LLP who with great interest and generosity agreed to represent me *pro bono* in a petition before the New York State Supreme Court requesting access to the records in the custody of Mr. Kendall with respect to the Germond case. Without the efforts of Mr. Kendall, Judge Rosenblatt and the Law Firm of McCabe & Mack LLP, the successful conclusion of this investigation would have been impossible. My initial inquiries began with back-and-forth conversations with the Dutchess County Chief Medical Examiner's Office Investigator Robert Brealy. Investigator Brealy finally advised me that records did exist but he is prevented from discussing them without a court order. Mr. Kendall was informed of the decision and through his professional interest and kindness, he made application on my behalf that was subsequently denied by the Court The petition was denied without prejudice Feb 15, 2018. As a result, a new petition was being arranged and I must await the signed Court Order from NYS Supreme Court Justice Christi J. Acker as of this writing (November 23, 2018)

Therefore, I leave my report where it is. I do not believe that any further evidence or documents will change my initial observations, but I am certainly, willing to do so if the evidence compels it.

The autopsy protocols and inquest minutes may reveal many answers to legitimate questions such as:

- The crime scene photos reveal a wound to the top of James Germond's skull that appears to me to not be an incised wound or a laceration but a type of blunt force injury indicating that the offender was able to get very close without much violence and the initial wound was not a stab wound – only the autopsy protocol would clarify that point,
- The location of all stab wounds is very important as well as their depth and measurement – including other injuries
- Any other evidence that may be held on the archival record
- The inquest minutes may very well make a case for perjury as the current record implies
- The actual clothing being worn by the victims at the time of autopsy can be extremely important
- There can be many other forensic implications contained in the archival records too lengthy to list here.

This is all that I can do with the evidence so far– CASE CLOSED (for now) The only answer left for me at this stage is litigation. As will be seen later some very generous people came forward to assist as my funds were depleting since I was now retired but dedicated to a conclusion of this case.

As like gifts from above, a government official, a law firm, a retired judge and the sitting District Attorney came forward and enabled me to proceed with litigation and a favorable outcome.

Who could have believed it?

CHAPTER **6**

Court Victory
Review of the Preserved Evidence

At Last, After Years of Research

On January 23, 2019 after about six years of research, I finally received a letter from my attorneys (McCabe & Mack LLP) that the New York State Supreme Court had granted me access to the Germond files. (See Exhibit #30) In addition, the decision of Judge Acker was forwarded as well and special thanks go to Hon. Albert M. Rosenblatt (McCabe & Mack) and Dutchess County Clerk, Bradford Kendall without whose help and kindness, I would be unable to continue this charitable research. (See Exhibit #'s 30, 30A & 30B)

I then began making arrangements to meet with Mr. Kendall to begin my review of the preserved evidence. After three years of searching and receiving very little assistance, I have located the Germond files referenced above. They are in the custody of the Dutchess County Clerk's Office Archives. As will be remembered, I was denied access initially for this non-profit undertaking. I then sought the assistance of the County Attorney and made a lengthy appeal in both the interests of justice and as an aid to future law enforcement in the examination of cold cases. My appeal was again denied and referred to the New York State Supreme Court. Keep in mind that this was a crime that occurred eighty-seven years ago, and is a purely charitable and

THE GERMOND FAMILY MURDERS

historical undertaking.

I then wrote a letter with extensive attachments to the New York State Supreme Court 9th District, Justice James Pagones. Again, my appeal for help was denied. I have absorbed all expenses from the past three years. The Judge would have me hire an attorney and pay him about five thousand dollars from my own pocket in order that he prepares a "formal application" to the court. I am retired and unable to expend any further expense. I did attempt to find a *pro bono* advocate, but this search was like finding a lost ring in the ocean.

On May 6, 2019 and for the next two weeks I began my review of the autopsy reports and inquest report as well as the retained District Attorneys file from 1933. Said review took place during this time period at the Dutchess County Clerk's Office, 22 Market Street, Poughkeepsie, New York and the Office of the Dutchess County District Attorney, 536 Main Street, Poughkeepsie, New York. Many thanks also to District Attorney William V. Grady for his assistance. I have tried to limit technical language to aid the reader of a better understanding. However, technical language is necessary in some cases in order to obviate a complete understanding. I have divided this final phase of my examination into the following categories:

1. Autopsy Reports
2. Inquest minutes
3. Suspects
4. DA's evidence
5. Crucial Affidavits
6. The Probable Offender
7. MY Conclusion

In this investigation I have read and reviewed 1274 pages of the inquest minutes another 450 pages of the District Attorneys case files about 400 pages of newspaper articles, two dozen crime scene photos and other physical evidence. Obviously, I can't cite everything but the most pertinent.

COURT VICTORY

The inquest reports are contained at the Dutchess County Clerk's Office. They are all bound and the reports are reproduced and attached to each autopsy report. They are in question-and-answer form and are type-written. I will add some significant bullet points from these many thousands of pages. Due to the length, it would not be practical to comment on all witness's testimony, some points are of interest:

- There was a great deal of talk about "The Willows Gun Club." However, I could find absolutely no evidence that this club had any substantive evidence to add to this case in the many thousands of pages of witness statements that I read,
- There was a constant preoccupation with the "Spaniards" in the area yet there was absolutely no evidence that the "Spaniards" had anything to do with this crime,
- Rumors ranged from the improbable to the utterly preposterous and most could be disproven by the existing evidence,
- As is normal in many investigations, times, dates and distances are under-stated or over-stated not in bad faith,
- There are numerous occasions of perjury never pursued by the authorities – discussed later,
- Numerous media accounts can be disproven,
- There is some fascinating inquest testimony in the reports that I will discuss later.
- There are over 200 witnesses who have testified and contained in question-and-answer form on the report of over 1300 pages – I have reviewed all of them.

Suspects

Steve Leko and Andrew Nemes

I have analyzed these suspects earlier and seeing nothing in the subsequently reviewed evidence to change that evaluation. However, due to the political nature of the crime, the investigation was turned over to the Governor's Office in 1932-33 and a major report was issued in the interrogation of Andrew Nemes, Jr. who had confessed and recanted that he had witnessed the crime.

The following generally describes the interrogation of Andrew Nemes in Albany, New York. Present: Andrew Nemes, Jr., Asa H. Arnold, Esq., Manning Cleveland, Esq. and Stenographer J.E. Finklestein.

The Interview was conducted by Hon. M. Muldin Fertig, Counsel to the Governor and Hugh Reilly, Esq., Assistant Attorney General. at the Capitol in Albany in room 208, December 13, 1932 from 2 P.M. to 6:50 P.M. The report is found in a bound booklet containing approximately 70 pages – I have read and analyzed the entire report as well as compared it to other evidence

Some general observations on this report. Mr. Nemes recounts accompanying Steve Leko to the Germond premises and witnesses the murder of the Germonds, not actually participating, but only witnessing as he was afraid of Mr. Leko. At this point, the report seems to be a very plausible scenario of the events but has a few problems. The forensic blood analysis is inconsistent with his story and the scenario is somewhat preposterous given Andrew's history as described earlier. Mr. Leko was never prosecuted in this case and the entire scenario seemed to be disregarded given the history of both subjects.

Paul Germond

Paul Germond became a suspect by mere inuendo of local residents who speculated that he was the target of the killings and the actual crime was a case of mistaken identity. There is absolutely no evidence anywhere on the record or in any of the thousands of documents that I have reviewed to connect Paul to this crime. In fact, there is evidence of probative value that he could not have committed this crime. Husted was seen alive at his farm at 4:30 P.M. having just left Paul's farm, two miles away, Paul would have needed a helicopter to go and come without his absence being noticed at his farm.

COURT VICTORY

The Man on the bus

I believe the "man on the bus" story is an absolute canard. He is off the bus at Willow Brook then travels two miles on foot to the Germond farm to kill Bernice who just enters the house where three other people are already dead. The found note together with this scenario are both preposterous on the facts.

The man walking on the highway

There is absolutely no evidence that this man has committed any crime. Moreover, the description of the three men in total all have varying descriptions. The local lore of this case sought to try to make them all one person. If these three men were all one and the same, it would require that he possess supernatural qualities.

The man in the store at Clinton Corners

This man sought a ride to Poughkeepsie and apparently made up some tales in order to gain sympathy for the purposes of obtaining a ride thereto. My evaluation of the two men that drove him stands as a classical Andy Warhol moment. The man was considered well-dressed. If he was the offender, he would have been covered with blood particularly on his shoes yet a clear description of his shoes appears on the record and no blood observed. He would have to have been carrying a change of clothes with him yet he had no luggage. Also, it is thought that finding Germond's wallet in the direction of Clinton Corners is further evidence that he was the offender. There is another very plausible and probative reason for an alternative explanation that follows.

Arthur Curry

See my initial evaluations and later combined with scientific evaluations.

THE GERMOND FAMILY MURDERS

Review of evidence continues – Poughkeepsie, New York - My Translations of the Forensic Pathology Data contained in the Autopsy reports

Autopsy Reports –

Mabel Germond

I have extensively reviewed the autopsy report of Mabel Germond from February, 1931 by Howard Carpenter, M.D., H.A. Richardson, M.D. and Coroner Paul G. Roberts. This was a particularly vicious assault and could easily be placed into a category known as a "rage assault." Mrs. Germond sustained five discernable knife wounds:

1. A 5 CM wound on the upper left breast, severing the sternum between rib #'s 2 & 3 then through the pericardium filling the sac with blood then lacerating the right auricle – MY NOTE: this is a wound that required excessive force since the sternum is the center breast plate (bone) with a descending cartilaginous growth known as the xiphoid process. The following wounds add to the ferocious nature of this assault and not the result of resistance to robbery but rather very personal in nature, (FATAL WOUND). In addition, there was no head wound on Mrs. Germond confirming my initial analysis of the crime scene photos.
2. A three-centimeter wound 6cm below the left nipple downward hitting the underlying rib.
3. A 3 cm wound downward and 6 cm below the left nipple 2 cm to the left inward and upward severing ribs 4&5 beyond the sternum entering the left lung at the base. MY NOTE: the wound sizes are consistent with the suspected knife and all wounds to the chest area indicate that she was being held as I have previously opined. Some wounds contradict my earlier report as upward wounds whereas I have opined that they

were upward wounds. In addition, some wounds were both penetrating as well as tearing wounds indicating a rather violent fight,
4. 6 cm wound of the posterior axillary line (side under right armpit) into the chest cavity penetrating the lower boarder of the upper lobe of the left lung – MY NOTE: this type of wound is incurred as they were fighting and she spun around – further proof that she was being held,
5. 3cm wound above the left ankle and inner surface of the leg downward and backward behind the tibia to make a wound of exit 4cm in length 4cm above the external malleolus (boney projection on either side of the ankle) – both chest cavities were filled with blood. This wound suggests a self-defense kicking attempt.

Much of these reports confirms most of which I had earlier opined.

Bernice Germond

I have examined the autopsy report of Bernice Germond conducted in February, 1931 by the same surgeons as before. Bernice sustained two serious (fatal) wounds and three non-fatal wounds:

1. 4cm stab wound below the clavicle (right) penetrating the chest wall between ribs 1 & 2 downward and inward penetrating the right lung.
2. Second wound similar to the 3cm wound above between ribs 3 & 4 downward and inward entering the pericardium to admitting three fingers and extending into the right auricle – pericardium sac filled with clotted blood – this wound in the right auricle continued through the septum (separates two upper chambers of the heart) and emerged through the left ventricle leaving a 1cm wound of exit. MY NOTE: fatal wound and further evidence of the rapidity of the strokes indicating Bernice was being held much the same as Mabel. It also

indicates to me that these two assaults occurred at different times – it would be hard to imagine that Bernice would have just stood there and watched all those horrific wounds being inflicted on her mother – blood evidence on crime scene photos refutes that possibility.
3. Non-fatal wound 4cm to the right of the first wound superficial in nature 2 cm at length at anterior border of the right deltoid, Non-fatal wound 4cm in length extending downward extending downward into the axilla (arm pit).
4. Non-fatal small stab wound right axilla 2cm in lengthBoth hands had deep incised wounds through the thenar eminence (base of the thumb on the palms) – blood on both hands. In addition, both chest cavities were filled with blood.

MY NOTE; wounds indicative of defense wounds and may indicate that there was a point when Bernice broke loose from her assailant. The hand wounds indicate the offender was striking in a downward motion as there were no lacerations to the inner metacarpals. (See Exhibit# 22, p. 133) One of the most important crime scene photos that apparently went undetected.

Raymond Germond

I have personally examined the autopsy report of Raymond Germond conducted in February, 1931 by the previously identified surgeons – there are six discernable wounds:

1. 4cm stab wound over the flexor surface of the right wrist which extended backward and upward beneath the ulnar leaving a wound of exit of 3cm – MY NOTE – these are usually wounds in flight or on one who is being concealed.
2. 3cm stab wound in length above the left clavicle downward and upward into the chest cavity to cross the midline – it incised the pericardium to the extent of 4cm wound of entrance and 2 ½ cm length in right auricle where it exited – pericardial

sac filled with clotted blood – both chest cavities were filled with blood, - fatal.
3. Stab wound 4cm in length in left axillary line and extended into the pectoral muscle with muscle hemorrhage.
4. Two superficial stab wounds over upper right chest at the level of #2 rib without penetration.
5. Another superficial wound over left chest at the level of #2 rib penetrating the pectoral muscle but did not enter the chest.
6. Another superficial wound 1cm over the lower border of the scapula towards the posterior axillary line – struck the bone and did not continue.

<u>MY NOTE</u> these wounds are consistent with the offender attempting to capture a small boy hiding under a wagon who is obviously a moving target – I would imagine his cries and screams would have alerted anyone who was still alive.

James Husted Germond

Unfortunately, the autopsy of Mr. Germond has been lost and an extensive search was conducted to locate it unsuccessfully. However, there is a comment in the inquest report of a witness who observed a wound to Mr. Germond's head which is consistent with my earlier observations of the crime scene photos whereas I have opined that he must have known the intruder to permit him to get that close after all the screaming he must have heard as he came to the scene. The wound on Mr. Germond's head, in my opinion, has the appearance of a blunt force injury other than a knife wound.

Evaluation of Autopsy Results

- I agree with the autopsy surgeons that the wounds are consistent with the recovered weapon,

- This was definitely a crime of rage by an offender who knew his / her victim and very unlike a crash-n robbery,
- My initial observations of the crime scene photos indicated a vertical thrust that is consistent with close-in assaults. However, the autopsy protocol clearly indicates a downward thrust and cutting of the wounds – these types of wounds are often seen when the perpetrator recovers the weapon from the victim,
- My blood pattern analysis (BPA) is entirely consistent with the autopsy findings,
- The fatal wounds in all three victims were the result of a pericardium penetration,
- Mrs. Germond's leg wound is consistent with a fight at the front door when she apparently tried to kick the offender,
- The superficial wounds are all indications of a direct violent assault on a victim who is resisting.
- Autopsy surgeons were able to fit recovered knife into wounds and opine that said knife was capable of producing the wounds.
- Also autopsy surgeons confirmed the blood on the knife was human blood,
- NOTE: at least this was a forensic effort and much more could have been done even then.

Inquest Reports

The inquest reports are contained at the Dutchess County Clerk's Office. They are all bound and the reports are reproduced and attached to each autopsy report. They are in question-and-answer form and are type-written. I will add some significant bullet points from these many thousands of pages. Due to the length, it would not be practical to comment on all witness's testimony,

- There was a great deal of talk about "The Willows Gun Club." However, I could find absolutely no evidence that this club

had any substantive evidence to add to this case in the many thousands of pages of witness statements that I read,
- There was a constant preoccupation with the "Spaniards" in the area yet there was absolutely no evidence that the "Spaniards" had anything to do with this crime,
- Rumors ranged from the improbable to the utterly preposterous and most could be disproven by the existing evidence,
- As is normal in many investigations, times, dates and distances are under-stated or over-stated not in bad faith,
- There are numerous occasions of perjury never pursued by the authorities – discussed later,
- Numerous media accounts can be disproven, There is some fascinating inquest testimony in the reports that I will discuss later.
- There are over 200 witnesses who have testified and contained in question-and-answer form on the report of over 1300 pages – I have reviewed all of them. There are also many separate affidavits.

At this point, a comparison of the evidence that was available at the beginning of this investigation and the evidence revealed after all available evidence was evaluated now seems appropriate. This is particularly significant with respect to the known suspects who became either deeply incriminated or totally exonerated. You will remember that all the evidence was not available to me until I had the Court Order granted to me by Judge Acker. As a matter of fact, the revealed evidence, together with the scientific analysis, virtually identifies the offender in this case.

The list of rumors and attached suspects amounted to dozens of individuals and even two groups. I have limited the most popular listing to the following because there was at least some "evidence" and witnesses (though of very weak probative value) attached to these parties.

Suspects

Since this investigation, I have received seemingly endless observations from people who have followed this case for many years. Most of the commentary centered on comments about the guilt of some of the witnesses that I have listed earlier. These commentaries suggest that there is evidence to suggest the culpability of one or more of the suspects identified. It should be noted that there are other suspects identified during the history of this case that I have not included in this investigation. It would have increased the length of this investigation and would have caused the number of pages in my report to be at least doubled. I can assure the reader that any suspects brought to my attention about which there was even a scintilla of evidence of probative value, were in fact investigated. Most of these were based on rumors and an attempt to connect convenient circumstances that were made to seem related to this case. One such example was the preposterous Connecticut connection.

Because of the volume of inquiries, I decided to revisit all the available evidence involving all of the suspects that I have identified herein. This included the 1400 pages of inquest minutes, my 690 pages of notes and commentary, the 575 pages of notes and affidavits contained in the District Attorney's files and about 500 pages of articles. I have even revisited the scenes where these claims were alleged to have taken place. Accordingly, I have found that my initial evaluation of the suspects stands as an accurate representation of the available evidence. In fact, this third re-examination reinforces my conclusions. Because this case can be complicated, I have chosen to repeat my evaluation of the evidence of these suspects as follows:

Steve Leko and Andrew Nemes

I have analyzed these suspects earlier and I see nothing in the subsequently reviewed evidence to change that evaluation. However, due to the political nature of the crime, the investigation was turned over to the Governor's Office in 1932-33 and a major report was issued in the interrogation of Andrew Nemes, Jr. who had confessed and recanted that he had witnessed the crime.

Present: Andrew Nemes, Jr., Asa H. Arnold, Esq., Manning Cleveland, Esq. and Stenographer J.E. Finklestein.

The Interview was conducted by Hon. M. Muldin Fertig, Counsel to the Governor and Hugh Reilly, Esq., Assistant Attorney General.

The interview was conducted at the Capitol in Albany in room 208, December 13, 1932 from 2 P.M. to 6:50 P.M.

The report is found in a bound booklet containing approximately 70 pages – I have read the entire report.

Observations – Mr. Nemes recounts accompanying Steve Leko to the Germond premises and witnesses the murder of the Germonds, not actually participating, but only witnessing – he was afraid of Mr. Leko. The report is a very plausible scenario of the events at first glance, but has a few problems. The forensic blood analysis is inconsistent with his story and the scenario is somewhat preposterous given Andrew's history as described earlier. Mr. Leko was never prosecuted in this case and the entire scenario seemed to be disregarded given the history of both subjects.

Paul Germond

Paul Germond became a suspect by mere inuendo of local residents who speculated that he was the target of the killings and the actual crime was a case of mistaken identity. There is absolutely no evidence anywhere on the record or in any of the thousands of documents that I have reviewed to connect Paul to this crime. In fact, there is evidence of probative value that he could not have committed this crime. Husted was seen alive at his farm at 4:30 P.M. having just left Paul's farm, two miles away, Paul would have needed a helicopter to go and come without his absence being noticed at his farm.

THE GERMOND FAMILY MURDERS

The Man on the bus

I believe the "man on the bus" story is an absolute canard. He is off the bus at Willow Brook then travels two miles on foot to the Germond farm to kill Bernice who just enters the house where three other people are already dead? The found note together with this scenario are both preposterous on the facts. Further, it should be noted that the probative evidence with respect to these suspects clarify most of these earlier impressions.

The man walking on the highway

There is absolutely no evidence that this man has committed any crime. Moreover, the description of the three men in total all have varying descriptions. The local lore of this case sought to try to make them all one person. If these three men were all one and the same, it would require that he possess supernatural qualities.

The man in the store at Clinton Corners

This man sought a ride to Poughkeepsie and apparently made up some tales in order to gain sympathy for the purposes of obtaining a ride thereto. My evaluation of the two men that drove him stands as a classical Andy Warhol moment. The man was considered well-dressed. If he was the offender, he would have been covered with blood particularly on his shoes yet a clear description of his shoes appears on the record and no blood observed. He would have to have been carrying a change of clothes with him yet he had no luggage. Also, it is thought that finding Germond's wallet in the direction of Clinton Corners is further evidence that he was the offender. There is another very plausible and probative reason for an alternative explanation that follows.

Arthur Curry

My initial evaluation of Mr. Curry's involvement in this case continues here from the earlier reports and impressions. There is nothing in the current evidence that alters my initial analysis except some minor timing issues. Moreover, the recovered evidence adds enormous weight to finding that Mr. Curry is the most probable offender. The written evidence as well as the forensic evidence has conclusively convinced me that Mr. Curry was a prodigious liar. It has been my professional experience over the past fifty-five years that offenders display certain undeniable proclivities. (see the "Vin Rules")

1. They tend to tell unnecessary lies because they are trying to disarm the investigators and the offender is not exactly certain just what the investigator already knows,
2. They try to conduct alternate scenarios for the investigators,
3. They will attribute things to sworn witnesses that those same witnesses will eventually deny,
4. They will construct alternate alibis as needed,
5. They love to talk and that is often their down fall.

These are often signs displayed by offenders in proximate homicide cases as well as major arsons and even terrorist events. Mr. Curry was indeed a true to form case example.

"Some" of the "Lies" of Arthur Curry

As I have noted earlier, offenders tend to tell unnecessary lies. In addition, lies must be consistent in that it is necessary to remember all the lies you tell in order to not get caught in a prevarication. Moreover, one's lies often unwittingly involve other witnesses who will be unable to corroborate the lies unless a conspiracy is entered into beforehand. The following very clearly demonstrates that Mr. Curry fell into all these traps and could have easily been discovered and prosecuted, many of his activities were themselves crimes including conspiracy, tampering with witnesses and numerous counts of perjury as previously described. Remember, many of his statements were under oath and some of the affidavits survive to this day.

THE GERMOND FAMILY MURDERS

Mr. Curry claimed that Mr. James Brennan, et al were present at his residence on Thanksgiving Eve 1930. A sworn affidavit by James Brennan refutes that claim and states that he was not present thereat. A sworn deposition by Ellis Robinson claimed that the victim's wounds at the crime scene were not visible and yet Mr. Curry was able to describe them to the police.

Mr. Curry stated that he was on the porch of his home at 6 PM on Thanksgiving Eve when he observed the regular bus stop in front thereat and was drawn to the attention of the squealing brakes causing him to turn on his lights. A sworn affidavit by Mr. John Edward Garrity states that he was the bus driver and that there were no squealing brakes and that he did not see Mr. Curry nor were his lights on. Furthermore, a sworn affidavit by Mrs. Hazel Johnson states that she was a passenger who got off in front of the Curry residence as she usually does and that there were no squealing brakes nor did she see Mr. Curry on his porch nor were the lights on. She remained thereat for fifteen minutes awaiting her father to pick her up.

Mr. Curry has denied stating that he cut Bernice's hair two days before the murder and that he stated that she had many boyfriends down in Poughkeepsie. A sworn affidavit by Mr. Charles Conger states that Curry did in fact make these statements to him and other statements regarding the connection that Bernice's friend may have been involved in the murder. NOTE: there are extensive affidavits on the record of Mr. Curry commenting on Bernice and the prospective motives for these crimes. For example, the extensive testimony under oath of Mr. Joseph Vail.

Mr. Curry testified that he entered the kitchen at the crime scene With Paul Germond. Mr. Paul Germond's sworn testimony states that Mr. Curry entered the kitchen first by himself against the warning of Mr. Germond who wanted to wait for the police.

NOTE: Mr. Curry made numerous recommendations as to how the investigation should proceed. For example, he recommended that a complete search of the surrounding woods and house should be conducted. Remember, the knife and wallet were found in the surrounding area. In addition, he was adamant about the knife not coming from inside the Germond house but "the knife came from outside." It was impossible for him to have known that.

NOTE: I have documented six counts of "flat out perjury" by Mr. Curry and one count of conspiracy to suborn perjury I have always been puzzled why a grand jury wasn't convened and indict him for homicide AND six counts of perjury. I believe the totality of the evidence if presented to the grand jury was adequate for at least probable cause but maybe not for "guilt beyond a reasonable doubt" which would be the standard for the homicides as well as perjury. He would almost certainly have been convicted of perjury.

The Major Evidence against Curry

In addition to all the evidence presented in the previous commentary, the following sworn affidavits are the most compelling:

1. The Sworn affidavits of <u>Jennifer Coffin</u> – she states that between 4:30 P, M, and 5 P.M. she saw a man whom she described as wearing the same clothes as Arthur J, Curry, the same height, slimness of build. At a later date she saw Arthur Curry in his clothes (she did not know Arthur Curry) and stated he resembled the man she saw on Germond property, November 26, 1930. The subsequent encounter occurred in the hallway with other men unknown to her as Curry was wearing the clothing he claimed to be wearing on the night of the crime. She further states that there was a light on in the kitchen when she first passed at between 4:30 and 5 P.M.

When she returned later at about 8 P.M., she did not see the light on in the kitchen.

2. The sworn statements and affidavits of <u>Raymond Buys and Mrs. Lillian Buys (his wife).</u> He stated that he entered the Curry home 10 minutes before Curry's arrival at about 6:45 P.M. and Mr. Buys arrival was at approximately 6:55 P.M. He noticed that Mr. Curry "Acted peculiar" in that he usually is in a hurry as Mr. Buys has been getting his hair cut there for six years. Mr. Curry was warming his hands at the stove for several minutes and when he later placed the towel around Buy's neck, his hands were quite cold. It was quite warm in the house and he has never witnessed Curry acting in this manner. Several days later Curry came to Mr. Buys house and ordered clam chowder which Buys had to open in cans since he was not accustomed to fresh clam chowder in his business (gas station),

3. At this visit, Curry sought to construct an alibi by claiming that Mr. Buys was there one hour earlier. Curry stated that "I guess we both have an alibi." Mr. Buys stated that Curry was a mean and rough and not a pleasant customer. Buys disliked him but has absolutely no animosity towards him. <u>Affidavits of Mrs. Lillian Buys</u> was very precise in the timing and corroborated Mr. Buys statement since they always had dinner and it was necessary that her son watch the store and relieve Mr. Buys and vice versa as the store closes at precisely 7:30 P.M. It should be noted that Mrs. Curry was confronted by the sheriff in the presence of Mr. Buys and she made a different statement than Mr. Buys claiming the arrival was earlier by one hour.

These sworn affidavits of Mr. and Mrs. Buys are so precise and corroborated their previous statements that these statements have high probative value.

COURT VICTORY

4. Sworn affidavit of <u>Mrs. Mary Orpha Curry</u> – she has in an earlier statement claimed that she rehearsed her testimony by being coached by Mr. Curry. She now recants it all and will testify truthfully as she was very afraid of Mr. Curry. She swears that Curry visited the Germond house hoping to get the money that was owed him as Curry was short of funds. On Thanksgiving Eve, November 26, 1930 at about 4:10 P.M. Curry left the house and stated he was going to the Germond's to get the money. Curry returned home about 10 or 15 minutes before Raymond Buys came in and that Curry hung up his coat and hat and washed his hands. She further confirms the totality of Mr. Buys sworn statement. She stated that Curry wore the same-colored clothes as earlier described by a number of witnesses. Curry then rehearsed the alibi with Mrs. Curry several times and stated to her "we know where we were, etc." she also swears that Mr. Curry is hot tempered and has an abusive attitude in general.
5. The sworn affidavit of <u>Hubert Schiffer</u> – testifies that about 5 or 10 minutes past 5, he passed the Germond property and noticed the lights on in Germond's truck and Germond walking through the yard towards the barn. He returned by the house again between 6:30 and 6:40 P.M. and saw a thin "lanky man" and claimed that the lights were all out – important evidence since it fits perfectly with Curry returning to his home just before the arrival of Raymond Buys.
6. The sworn testimony of <u>Miss Grace Brennan</u> – Curry testified that he called Miss Brennan to confirm that Mrs. Hazel Johnson did get off the bus at 6:15 in front of his house. Miss Brennan swore under oath that she never had any phone conversations with Curry and he definitely did not call her up.
7. The sworn testimony of <u>Mr. Ford Friedah</u> – testifies that Curry stated that Bernice was a "hot natured girl" and he was "up against an awful thing." Moreover, Mr. Friedah testified that he has sold brown gloves identical to those found at the crime

scene but has never sold such gloves to Mr. Germond. Curry has denied these statements.

8. Sworn testimony of <u>Mr. Dennis Haggerty</u> who swears under oath that he is the bus driver who picked up Bernice Germond in Poughkeepsie and dropped her off in front of her home at exactly 5:20 P.M. on November 26, 1930. He is so precise because of his role as a driver whereas timing is an important part of his work and he always checks. Bernice usually smiles at him when leaving the bus and always says good night in a very pleasant voice. This night she did not. When she started to get off the bus, she seemed startled and stared directly at the house for a couple of minutes and then walked slowly towards the house without saying a word. There were some early reports that she said "the house is all dark I guess no one is home." This may have been a 1930 statement but it is not contained in the 1933 affidavit and testimony. However, Mr. Haggerty was very adamant about Bernice's strange behavior.

There are many other affidavits and testimony on the record upon which one could opine – I chose the ones with the most probative value.

The Case Against Arthur J Curry

Of all prospective suspects, Mr. Curry is the only one who fits the description of the man observed in the Germond driveway. In law, there is a notion called "consciousness of guilt." This can be shown in numerous ways. Construction of alibis, flight, remaining at the scene and making recommendations, advancing arguments to defer guilt, prevaricating conversations that others can't recall. Mr. Curry fits all these proclivities on multiple occasions.

COURT VICTORY

He attempted to construct an alibi with several people such as Raymond Buys and his own wife, et al. He made statements that were provably false about Bernice Germond He attempted to direct the investigation to an outsider. I must note that he was somewhat successful in this regard, He named numerous witnesses who under oath denied what he claimed including visitors at his home, His time line was provably false as demonstrated in my opening analysis, He made endless recommendations on the direction of the investigation including that the whole vicinity should be searched including "all the woods" – it should be noted here that the wallet was found in a culvert easily observable from the road and the knife was discovered in the opposite direction 75 feet from the house in the direction of Rt. 82. It should be noted further that both locations were easily accessible to Curry completely undetected.

He had easy flight as will be shown by azimuth readings and software at the County Clerk's office (See Exhibit # 11). A distance of .46 miles and 1231 feet in a hypotenuse measurement. I walked on the road from the Curry house to the Germond house in 6 minutes and 40 seconds staying totally on the road. Cutting through the fields and over the Wappingers Creek reduced that time greatly and avoids any form of detection.

Curry was quite adamant in his insistent claim that the knife did not come from inside the house. I have opined at length earlier on this issue. Most of the issues on which I have opined have been shown to be accurate and the crime scene evidence sustains the belief in an offender with rage.

Experiments have shown that three of the murders could easily have been accomplished in 15 minutes even if Mr. Germond is observed in the driveway at 5:05 PM and Bernice arrives at 5:20 as the final victim, The additional time left to accommodate his arrival home at 6:45 gave him more than enough time to plant the wallet, pass through the woods and remove any bloody clothing and clean up.

His efforts to slander Bernice Germond are almost neurotic. Numerous affidavits contain his suggestions that it was Bernice's flirtatious conduct that was the cause of the crime, if that were so, then why was Bernice killed last?

If there still exists any doubt in the minds of any investigator or reader as to whether Bernice was killed last, I call your attention to an overlooked piece of evidence by the original and subsequent investigators from the original crime scene photos. As already demonstrated by the evidence, the famous "Brown gloves" were worn by the offender. Look closely at crime scene photo Exhibit #22. These gloves are laying on the very table under which the body of Bernice finally came to rest. The interpretation is obvious. It reminds one of the old Casey Stengel adage: "you can observe a lot just by watching."

For nearly six decades, I have participated in the investigation and questioning of witnesses. As a result, I have developed some very basic alerts when questioning people. For all you investigator "wannabees," I call these alerts "The Vin Rules."

I thought it would be appropriate for all the commentators on this case, private investigators, lawyers and authors to take a little time here to make some tutorials on criminal investigations and evaluating witnesses. Accordingly, I offer these thirty observations gleaned over many decades of talking to and interrogating many hundreds of witnesses.

"The Vin Rules:"

Rule #1 – When people start doing something that they never do, or stop doing something that they always do, there must be a reason,

Rule #2 - Guilty people always tell unnecessary lies,

Rule #3 – The first story you hear is usually the wrong one,

Rule #4 – Guilty people often peddle distant theories and mysterious offenders,

Rule #5 - Never commit yourself to the old adage that "the criminal always returns to the scene of the crime," More likely, the criminal never leaves the scene of the crime.

Rule #6 – A witness may not really be a witness. Break witnesses down into three categories: first, the interested witness; secondly, the disinterested witness and thirdly, the Andy Warhol witness seeking his "fifteen minutes of fame."

Rule #7 – No person can tell the same lie the exact same way three times in a row.

Rule #8 – A rumor has no value as evidence and rarely leads to evidence of probative value.

Rule #9 – Reputation by itself, depending upon the case, rarely identifies the offender.

Rule #10 – If man A wants to kill man B, man B will die.

Rule #11 – The one thing in this world that's truly "on the level" is professional wrestling.

Rule #12 – Just because "it" says so doesn't mean it is.

Rule #13 - If "its" not there, "its" gone.

Rule #14 – Good intentions will not change reality.

Rule #15 – They don't payoff for almost.

Rule #16 – When someone says "to be quite honest with you" or words to that effect, he has just told or is about to tell a lie.

Rule #17 – The "Devil's Advocate" is usually the devil.

Rule #18 – People who answer questions with questions are usually guilty of something.

Rule #19 – Seeing and believing have nothing in common.

Rule #20 – If sense was so common, everybody would have it.

Rule #21 – Never trust a person who answers a question you didn't ask.

Rule #22 – "Reputation is rarely proportioned to virtue"

Rule #23 – Flattery is the favored weapon of the cynic or the guilty.

Rule #24 – Your boss is always with you, win or tie.

Rule #25 – A picture is not worth a thousand words as evidence alone.

Rule #26 – If all you have is a confession, you've got nothing.

Rule #27 – Superstition is like luck; it is a misunderstanding between cause and effect.

Rule #28 - You can always tell a survivor, he's the one who'd rather be wrong than quoted.

Rule #29 – You know you're talking to an arrogant person if he thinks that God would agree with him if He only had all the facts.

Rule #30 – Yogi Berra, Tom Lasorda and Casey Stengel belong on Mt. Rushmore.

It is indeed ironical that almost all of the "Vin Rules" certainly rang true in this Case. Mr. Curry can be used as a training model for the "Vin Rules."

CHAPTER 7

Conclusions & Acknowledgements Missing Parts?

Concluding Opinions

This work would not be complete without a summary of my findings on this case and why, strictly from a forensic point of view, that I have opined on the final solution in this case. There are very discernable and probative reasons why I have arrived at the solutions that are described below

All the actions and conduct of Mr. Curry have been carefully documented through sworn testimony on the record and even his own words. Also, there is forensic evidence with respect to timing, spatial considerations, physical capacity, etc. that lend themselves to a reasonable conclusion. In addition, it was critical to disprove many of the theories and eliminate suspects using the same logic. Key among the definitive findings that forensic typologies use in weighing evidence:

- Mr. Curry was the only person to have any need to remove the bodies form the barnyard since he was the only person who could have known that the bus would stop in front of the Germond home at 5:20 P.M. because he lived at that very intersection and watched the same bus stop there for a number of years. The bodies had to be removed or Bernice or anyone on the bus could have seen them thereby hampering his flight. Moreover, Bernice had to be murdered when she entered the house as she would have discovered. both Mr. Curry and the body of her mother.

- Mr. Curry made endless efforts on the sworn record to enlist other persons to aid him in an alibi; all of whom denied his attempts at an alibi and some even claiming that they never conferred with him. This pattern has been shown time again to match to persons who are guilty who also often tell "unnecessary lies."

- Mr. Curry devoted nearly two years after the murder to marketing the notion that a romantic interest in Bernice was the cause and an outside suitor committed this crime. He went so far as to swear under oath that he stated that he had two conversations with Bernice prior to the murder that he later denied. Two sworn witnesses stated that he did make those statements. I believe that he even convinced an assistant prosecutor that Bernice was the basis of this crime.

- His conduct at the crime scene was entirely suspicious. He claimed that he entered the house with another person when in fact that person stated under oath that he did not. He insisted that the area be searched for evidence and claimed that the knife came from outside the house. He had absolutely no way of knowing that. He also made later claims about the injuries that he could not possibly have known.

- He has conspired with his wife to validate his time in the house at the time of the crime and even enlisted a haircut customer to assist him. The perjured testimony of Mr. Curry and his wife are documented on the record and repudiated later under examination.

CONCLUSIONS & ACKNOWLEDGEMENTS

- Mr. Curry has a documented propensity for violent acts in the past as was evident from the testimony of both his son and Mrs. Curry. Other witnesses have sworn under oath as to his violence. Also, Mr. Curry served a prison term in Sing Sing Penitentiary in Ossining, New York for assault and was under investigation at the time for another assault. This background is consistent with my early analysis that this was a crime of violence and also consistent with basic forensic typologies.

It should also be pointed out that the offender is not likely to have deposited evidence of the crime in two opposite directions. Why would the offender walk out of the house and walk completely around the house, risking detection, and throw the knife in the opposite direction from where the wallet was found? The only possible reason was to confuse the authorities of the direction of flight thereby eliminating a local suspect. Especially a suspect who lived literally across the road. It is however only a local suspect who would have staged these pieces of evidence in such a fashion. Moreover, there is a great deal missing in this case. The missing autopsy report of Mr. Germond for example. This report had enormous value since I believed that it would have proven my observation of two crime scene photos of Mr. Germond's body. The photo shows bleeding in an even trail from the top of the head to the base of the chin. It is my opinion that this wound is inconsistent with a knife wound and more consistent with a blow to the head. I am persuaded that this report would have shown that a person well-known to Mr. Germond was able to get very close to him particularly after being summoned by his son that a fight with his wife was in progress at the house.

All the clothing from all the victims has not been preserved. Some of the clothing was preserved but like the rest of this case, many amateur detectives have been permitted to pick over the evidence over the years and obviously remove most of it. I was shocked to find the crime scene photos still in place. You might be wondering what good this old evidence could contribute to this case today. Well, you'd be surprised. For example, all the victims clothing could still be subjected to DNA analysis and blood analysis. It would be unlikely, but possible, that DNA could be recovered in a meaningful profile even in mitochondrial format. However, blood evidence is more residual and it was possible to surveil for blood evidence using any number of modern techniques. The newspaper seen on the table, silverware in the house, the famous gloves, etc. could all be subjected to modern analysis. We could learn a great deal even from the cuts on the gloves and garments. Fingerprints have been detected on many surfaces many years after their discovery; this is not news. There is absolutely no record on the retained evidence of Mr. Curry's garments having been subjected to even minimal blood screening.

There is a rather *sub rosa* aspect to this case and it involves potential corruption. The interrelationships in this case with the suspect and law enforcement in this case cannot be overstated. We have Mr. Curry as a former deputy sheriff and he is involved in the weddings of some of these players together with socializing at Mr. Curry's home and many other instances of a lack of distancing from interested parties in this case not to mention suspicion about Mr. Curry's activities as both a gambler and bootlegger. Though I found no evidence of probative value of any misconduct, perhaps a contemporary inquiry would have revealed a more startling nexus. One can't help but notice that it took nearly three years to seriously consider Mr. Curry a suspect. In addition, there existed rather clear probable cause to believe that Mr. Curry may have committed perjury, conspiracy and tampering with witnesses. There are actually sworn affidavits that would form the gravamen of such probable cause. The fact there is no surviving police memoranda of interrogations and observations maybe explained to the passage of time and amateur investigators removing those documents does not fully explain their total absence from the surviving official record. Fortunately, sworn witness statements have survived.

It is my professional opinion that Mr. Curry is the most probable offender based on many factors including his post-crime conduct, endless lies, construction of unnecessary alibis for one innocent of

CONCLUSIONS & ACKNOWLEDGEMENTS

a crime, his very background and behavioral history, his post-crime investigative recommendations, etc. and all of the other substantive issues already reported and developed in this case.

It may seem like I'm being unfair to the law enforcement and prosecutors at the time of this crime. The fact is that I am quite sympathetic to the complex nature of this investigation and even contemporary investigations of this type. However, I simply cannot dismiss some very basic mishandling of this case that was even known to most all law enforcement personnel and prosecutors around the world at the time of this crime. Surely, securing the crime scene, crime scene sketches, orderly searches, coordination of witnesses, order of interrogations, fixing investigative authority just to name a few. None of these very basic activities took place as well as the preservation of already obtained evidence.

I disagree with the judicial handling of this case as well as the law enforcement conduct. Mr. Curry could have been indicted based on circumstantial evidence of murder even if it was perceived that he could not be found guilty beyond a reasonable doubt. Moreover, he could have easily been indicted and convicted of at least six counts of "flat-out" perjury as well as one count of conspiracy to suborn perjury as well as tampering with witnesses. I am willing to review any other evidence should any exist but I seriously doubt that it would change any of the findings nor cause me to opine on a different conclusion. As far as I am concerned, this case is closed. I did all that I could.

This case could not have been completed without the generosity and cooperation of a number of interested parties. In addition, there will remain unnamed those who not only showed no interest in finding the truth, but also took no reasonable effort at the most minimal level of cooperation.

We didn't hear the end of Mr. Curry after his case was dismissed and the District Attorney failed to prosecute him for the other crimes that he committed during this investigation. Mr. Curry sued for false arrest but the case was dismissed on the face of the complaint. You have to give Mr. Rosen (Curry's lawyer) kudos for his boldness in litigating a false arrest claim by a man who had committed numerous other crimes in addition to the murder charge for which he was arrested.

After the case was fundamentally over, with respect to Mr. Curry, it became quite evident that the Pinkertons' initial analysis was correct from the beginning of their enlistment in the case. The initial Pinkerton investigators opined that the crime was committed by a person known to the victims and that the weapon's origin was from inside the Germond residence. Moreover, they were the only persons who had the order of killings correctly defined and the subsequent forensic evidence would prove them to be absolutely right. If that point of view would have been adopted right from the beginning, it is my view that the case would have had its greatest chance for a solution.

It was later discovered that Mr. Curry had lied about his place of birth for a number of years during his 17-year residence in Stanfordville. He claimed to have been born in Fonda and / or Rome, New York. In reality, he was born in Ontario, Canada and moved to Fonda at the age of 9 years. The District Attorney had a copy of his birth certificate in the files that I have researched and I have reviewed an actual copy of his birth certificate at the District Attorney's Office as part of my work product in this case.

Mr. Curry was not a citizen but was allowed to vote in all local elections. It is not clear from the surviving record what was the extent of knowledge concerning this fact. However, Mr. Curry was a candidate for Justice of the Peace and even ran for Town of Stanford Supervisor. Keep in mind as well that Mr. Curry was once a Deputy Sheriff.

The Curry home was the accepted meeting place for lawyers, politicians, public officials, community leaders and law enforcement. Routine parties and other local functions were held there. It is my position that this conviviality with all these "movers and shakers" formed the basis of the delay in considering Mr. Curry as a suspect. It took nearly three years to seriously consider Mr. Curry despite endless issues that were quite obvious at the time particularly many of

CONCLUSIONS & ACKNOWLEDGEMENTS

his "misstatements."

His background seemed to be well concealed from the general public that both the judge and the prosecutor were not aware of Mr. Curry's confinement for felonious assault in Sing Sing State Penitentiary. This knowledge seems to have been discovered just months before the hearing in 1933.

There is some evidence on the record that friends of Mr. Curry began to promote the notion of the involvement of Steve Leko in this crime. Law enforcement tended to doubt Leko's involvement in the crime, though he was interrogated and confined at length. A large amount of this doubt came from the claims of Andrew Nemes. Andrew concocted and repudiated his claims about Mr. Leko on several occasions including affidavits taken in Albany, New York by state prosecutors. Andrew's I.Q. hovered around 70 and some of his claims could easily be disproven. Moreover, Steve Leko was 4'11" and weighed 104 lbs. It did not escape law enforcement that Leko wasn't much bigger than Raymond Germond and he would be considered tiny when compared to Husted and Mabel Germond. Accordingly, it was quietly perceived that this crime would have been quite a gymnastic fete for Steve Leko even in his best physical day. As one investigator said "possible but very highly unlikely."

There are many stories, theories and rumors that I have uncovered in this investigation that I have chosen to exclude from this book. For example, old clothes were uncovered buried in a field near the crime scene and many thought that this was the break in the case. However, the record reflects that these clothing were subjected to "tests" and found not to be pertinent to this case. The description of these "tests" was not recorded so I have no way to comment on the probative value of the evidence. I must conclude that adequate inquiry was made that caused this evidence to be excluded. I have no way to know for certain.

Several jilted lovers came forward to make claims about their partners during the three-year course of this case. They all, one way or another, accused their lover of the murders. Even a Connecticut woman came forward with what seemed significant claims. She knew a great deal about the case and for a time was taken seriously. However, after serious inquiry, he was "totally" eliminated as a suspect.

One of the reasons that so many theorists and "witnesses" came forward was the confusion in investigative findings by law enforcement who seemed to change their theories of the crime regularly. It is my belief that if law enforcement had arrived at a solid theory of the events, then this case would have had a greater chance of solution much faster.

One of my initial techniques in the investigation was to try to eliminate suspects. This was much easier than I thought it would be, When I became reasonably familiar with the evidence, I discovered that almost anybody could become a suspect. Many were taken seriously by law enforcement because they had no clear scenario of the crime. Therefore, based on my forensic experience alone, many suspects were eliminated as either lacking credibility or their claims were even preposterous. It did come down to elimination but I was not only unable to eliminate one suspect, I discovered evidence of probative value that amounted almost to "probable cause" as to his involvement.

One really didn't require a degree in forensic science to reach some of the conclusions in this case. Logic would have sufficed. For example, the primary suspect in this case for at least two years was the famous foreigner who appeared in Oakleigh Robinson's store in Clinton Corners at 8 P.M the night of the crime. If this man is to become your prime suspect, then the following questions must be posed:

- Why would a stranger kill three people for no reason at all then wait around then kill the fourth person for clearly no reason instead of trying to escape?
- Why would a man stab four people 23 times and drag two bodies across a barn yard obviously covered with blood from head to foot and wander around a main roadway inviting detection?

CONCLUSIONS & ACKNOWLEDGEMENTS

- And how could that same man wander in the open down that road for 3 1/2 miles 2 1/2 hours after the crime and have no interest in detection?
- How could a well-dressed man enter that grocery store, make several purchases, speak to at least four people who did not notice any marks or blood stains? Make up a "cock and bull story" to get a ride to Poughkeepsie and apparently know some local names? How could this man be the killer?

It should always be kept in mind that there are different kinds of witnesses. The best kind of witness is the "disinterested witness" who have no dog in the fight. There is another kind and that is the Andy Warhol witness who actually internalizes his involvement and tends to confirm other commentaries. This is in fact, his "fifteen minutes of fame." All of the main witnesses in this case with one exception, are truly disinterested and have signed sworn affidavits. This type of witness has the highest probative value.

CHAPTERS **8 – 9ff**

Explanations & Exhibits

THE FOLLOWING EXHIBITS are not the totality of the evidence that I have collected. This book is intentionally reduced in size to allow for unstudied readers the ability to refer back and forth on numerous issues. You will also find repetition in this work and that is intentional since many of the concepts and issues are both complex and confusing. You will also note that I have selected cover descriptions for all the included photographic evidence for explanative purposes as well as to demonstrate the nexus between the photo and some proof issues about which I opine throughout.

Most of the attachments (not all) were taken from surviving crime scene photos preserved at the Dutchess County Sheriff's Office and are publicly available and found throughout publications and made available over the years by the Sheriff's Office. High intensity iPhone camera photos were enhanced for clarity and are retained by your humble investigator. However, initially it was far too costly to provide each recipient of my work with pristine photographic copies. As a result, I have photo copied the originals and attached them to the basic report and used in this book. They are at least adequate for this purpose. The forensic and evidentiary value is not lost in these reproductions. However, the original reproductions would be the most adequate and appropriate for testimonial or in-court presentation to be used as evidence, however, they are more than adequate for the

EXPLANATIONS & EXHIBITS

purposes of this inquiry. I evaluated the originals and they have enabled some of my opinions without defect.

It is not known if this is the totality of all crime scene photos, but it is the total being retained at the Dutchess County Sheriff's Office. I welcome hearing from anyone who has other evidence that can be forensically evaluated. I will do so and opine without fee. It should also be noted that I will NOT send any addendums to this work including hard copies of my final official report or the work product therefrom. Also, I will not forward any additional crime scene photos nor autopsy reports as they are somewhat graphic, and I wish to respect the sensitivities of any reader who may offense from such a display as well as full compliance with the orders of the Court.

NOTE: reasonably extensive inquiry has been made to determine if any relatives or witnesses survive within the first degree of kindred. As of December 31, 2015, none have been located. It should also be noted that there are notations in the autopsy protocols that I have chosen not to publish as they tend to create a misunderstanding in the minds of most readers who are not well trained in forensic pathology.

There were seemingly endless leads and other issues that popped up over three years. In fact, they continue even to this day by older residents of the area. Many of the leads had nothing to do with this case. As a matter of fact, law enforcement spent months investigating two issues involving guns. The first gun was a revolver owned by the Germond family that disappeared after the crime was discovered. There are endless newspaper accounts until finally it was discovered that a person who appeared at the crime scene absconded with the revolver. The name of this person is nowhere in the surviving record.

The other gun was an illegal weapon owned by Arthur Curry. Law enforcement was aware of the existence of this weapon and obtained a search warrant for Curry's home to search for it. They found it and charged Curry with illegal possession of the gun. The final disposition of this matter is not to be found in the surviving records. It should be pointed out that the accounts of these two events are from newspaper accounts and are not in the surviving record. There was apparently an immense amount of time and investigative resources devoted to these two issues. These were issues that really had absolutely nothing to do with the solution to this crime. Would that the same amount of time and investigation resources had been spent on the murder case, an entirely different outcome may have been possible.

The most significant lead occurred in a newspaper account in the Poughkeepsie Eagle concerning buried clothing found in a field not far from the murder scene. The article indicated that the clothing was turned over to law enforcement who "tested" the clothing. Nothing else was reported on this finding and there are no official surviving records to substantiate this matter. I find this piece very suspicious. Finding buried clothing near the scene of a multiple murder, is at least, a very important matter and the extent of the investigation and follow up testing, should be fully reported. After all, who would throw away old clothing by taking them out in the field and bury them? Everything had use in those days and few things except garbage were not saved. Old boards, scrap metal and clothing were maintained for future use, particularly clothing as patches and rags.

Missing Parts

What could have been done by law enforcement on November 26, 1930 that may have obviated a solution to this case long ago? Here is a small list:

- Saved and preserve all the clothing of all the victims as well as all suspects,
- Obtain a search warrant for Mr. Curry's home and grounds,
- Further preservation and analysis of all crime scene evidence for future testing as forensic science was in a developmental stage,
- Mr. Germond's autopsy report should have been preserved and safeguarded as with all other evidence to prevent unauthorized persons from having access to the evidence,

- Maintain comprehensive written reports of all actions taken in furtherance of the investigation,
- Experts in the field should have taken complete control of this case given the fact that on scene Law enforcement and even lawyers had literally no homicide investigative experience,
- ABOLUTELY SECURE THE CRIME SCENE IMMEDIATELY,
- Prepare proper crime scene sketches,
- Enlist trained and experienced interrogators.
- Slavishly observe the "Vin Rules" described earlier

I recognize that it seems that I am being unduly harsh on the law enforcement personnel at the time of this crime but the above issues were very basic law enforcement techniques even then in Dutchess County, New York. It was certainly the protocol of the New York State Police at that time. However, it seems as though both the State police and others tried to distance themselves from this case as the locals seemed to be running about without guidance or leadership following every rumor and even creating rumors themselves. Once the case was turned over to lawyers from New York State, politics and amateurism was the order of the day.

As a final point, having spent several years looking at all this evidence and studying the record, I am unable to exclude certain levels of seeming corruption in this case. The absolutely puerile handling of this investigation, both at the time of the crime, and thereafter, tells a partial story of willful blindness.

Dedication and Thanks

THERE ARE NUMEROUS professionals that I would like to thank for helping me and there are a number of persons who tried to hinder me. I'd like to concentrate on the ones that helped me. I must start with Ginny Buechele, noted Dutchess County historian whose professional contributions to the body of historical knowledge in this area are too numerous to list, Ginny gave me some initial advice and places to start that turned out to be most helpful.

I then came in contact with Sgt. Jonathan Hughes, Records Officer, Dutchess County Sheriff's Office in Poughkeepsie, New York. Jonathan invited me to inspect the remaining files and crime scene photos at the Sheriff's office. He was instrumental to my initial research and if one wished to make a list of truly professional police officers, the name of Jonathan Hughes would be near the top of the list. His staff was also quite convivial and most helpful.

Bradford Kendall is the Dutchess County Clerk whose assistance in leading me to other decision makers and finding me a litigation team made this investigation possible. I must admit that without Brad, this case would not have advanced. I am also pleased to note that Mr. Grady and Brad Kendall have been recently reelected to their posts by the people of Dutchess County, New York. Both the staffs of Mr. Grady and Mr. Kendall were most gracious and helpful. A great vote of thanks to Hon. Albert Rosenblatt, whose kindness and devoted interest in the historical record cannot be ignored. In addition, Judge Rosenblatt introduced me to his law firm, McCabe & Mack, LLP, who

EXPLANATIONS & EXHIBITS

graciously represented me before the court *pro bono* and to their staff.

In fidelity to the facts, I must state that there were those who not only refused to help in this undertaking but actually tried to hinder my progress. It was indeed surprising that those that I expected to help were the most unhelpful. They included newspapers, magazine writers, some senior law enforcement personnel and other commentators. When I contacted them and advised them that various publications that they had advanced over the years have now had much of their worked forensically explained.

I found that correcting the record after ninety years was no small task.

I never intended to write this book and I've told many people that I only wanted to do a report so that other professionals could benefit from my work. However, I received many inquiries on this case and other professionals found the case so fascinating and coincidental that writing a book was the only solution.

Disclaimer

The attached exhibits (photos) herein are taken from the public record. No documents nor exhibits derived from the documents and exhibits authorized for analysis and inspection by the Court Order have been reproduced here or elsewhere as per the Order of the Court. The author has merely opined on the contents of these documents with respect to their scientific and probative value.

EXPLANATIONS & EXHIBITS

EXHIBIT #1

The Cookingham Family, as previously reported, were early settlers of the Dutchess County area, then originally known as the Nine Partners Tract in the sixteenth century. They were dairy farmers originally from Germany and raised Holsten Dairy Cattle. The attached photo demonstrates the family's early activities and the use of red barns. A similar styled red barn (not the one in the photo) was situated across from my grandparents' home in Stanfordville. The home is now a refurbished home and currently used as a residence on the banks of Wappingers Creek. It was once known as "Ben Wheeler's Feed" after its initial use as both a dairy and hay barn. I can still clearly remember sitting by the creek and watching the grain and feed being loaded and off loaded as well as the various smells of the feed and grain

THE GERMOND FAMILY MURDERS

Near Hull

Primrose Hill Farm

Home   History   Directions   Tree Care   Contact Us

The History of Primrose Hill Farm:

The Cookingham family came to America from Wurttemburg, Germany in the 1730's during the Palatine Emigration. They settled on this property in a small house on the northeast corner of the 120 acre property in an area known as "Rocky Daniel". Primrose Hill Farm's name has been in use since 1867 when it first appeared in Beer's Atlas of New York and Vicinity. The current farmhouse was built in 1854 when Michael Cookingham and his wife, Abigail Harris, were married. They were great-grandparents of Viola Cookingham (Schoch), the current owner, who was born in the living room of the house.

The farm is one of the few remaining farms in Dutchess County which has remained in the same family for well over one hundred years. The farm was operated as a general family farm with cows, chickens, horses, pigs and an orchard by Harlow C. Cookingham until 1957. The first Christmas trees were planted in 1963.

The barn is an authentic Dutch bank barn built in the 1700's with three floors. The structure is made of handhewn oak beams.

In 1933, a beacon light was installed on the farm's hill as a navigational aid for aircraft traveling from Montreal to New York City and operated nightly until the advent of radar.

The Fiddler's Bridge Road Legend:

Local legend tells of an old fiddler who played his fiddle for festivals and dances throughout northern Dutchess County. On September 7, 1808, while trudging home at night along a narrow dirt road between Pleasant Plains and Schultzville, he was robbed and murdered. When he failed to return home, people went looking for him and found his body under the bridge. The old wooden bridge rotted long ago and a replacement was named Fiddler's Bridge in memory of the old fiddler. More recently, the road connecting Pleasant Plains and Schultzville has been named Fiddler's Bridge Road. In 1992, a town sign was placed to mark the spot where the stream still flows. On certain moonlit nights, the fiddler's ghost can be heard playing still!

EXPLANATIONS & EXHIBITS

EXHIBITS 1A1, 1A2, 1A3

Historic Immigration documents and voyage of Margaret (Fallon) Cookingham to the United States from Ireland and then to Stanfordville, New York

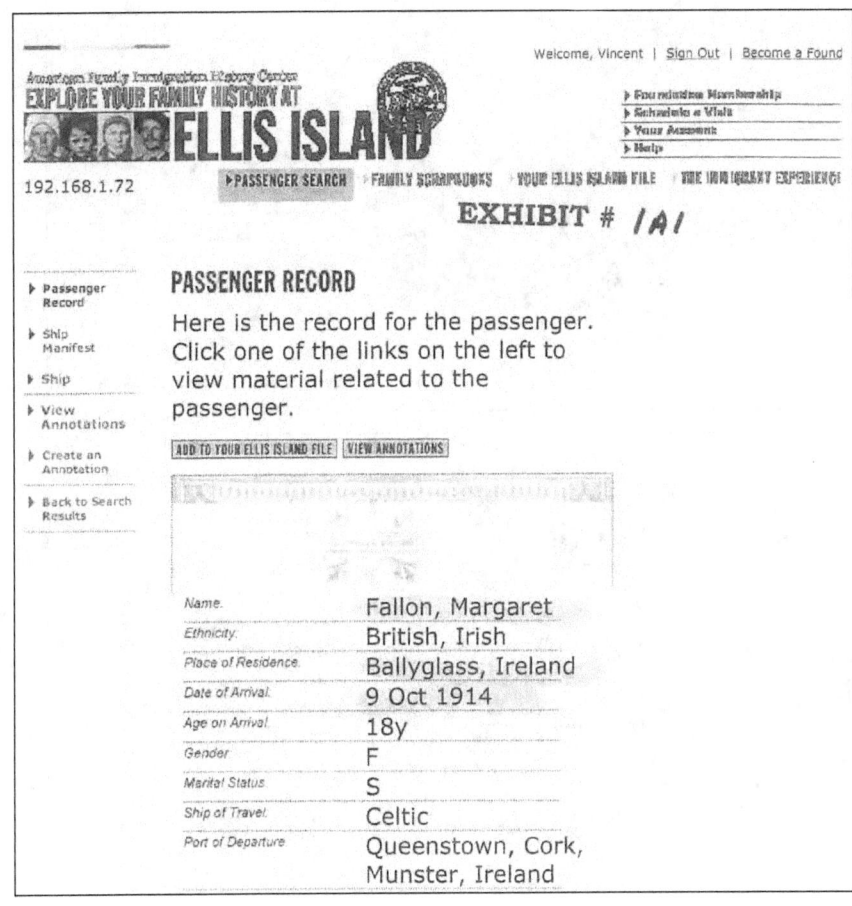

THE GERMOND FAMILY MURDERS

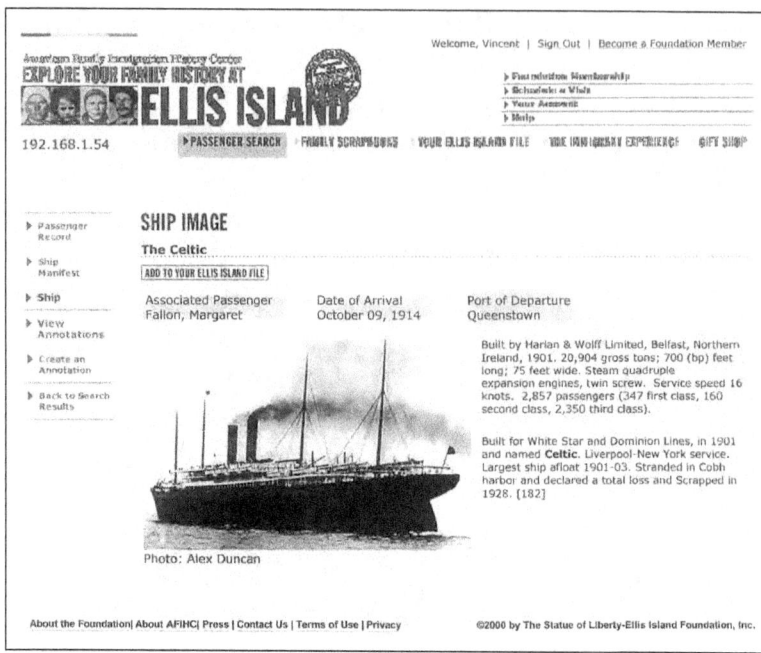

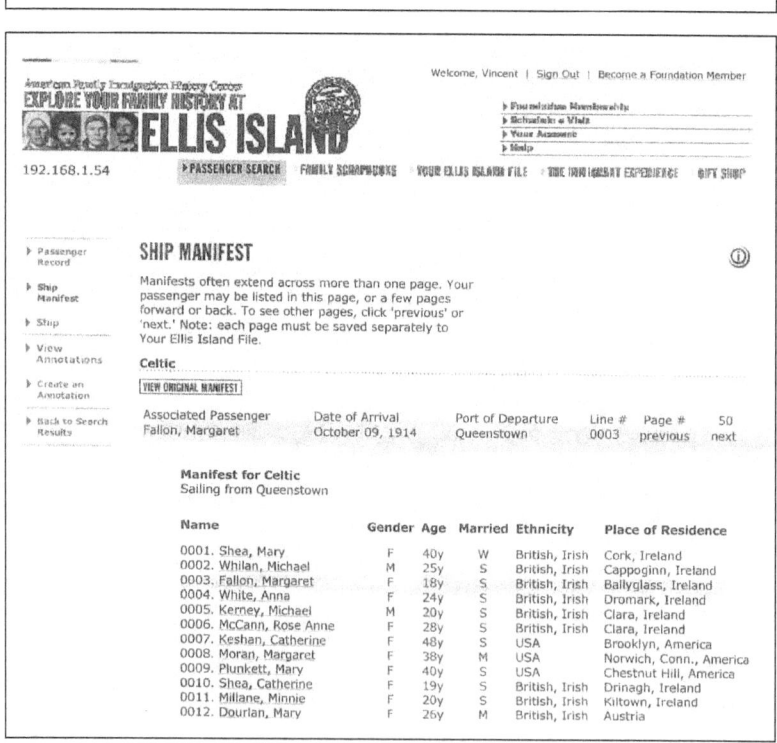

EXHIBIT #2 &2A

The two attached sketches give the reader some idea of the crime scene and the recovery of evidence. Two important points will become obvious: first the entire area involving this crime is rather proximate and has been greatly exaggerated by writers over the years. Secondly, the subsequent recovery of the evidence was accomplished by non-law enforcement personnel and told a far larger narrative than assumed at the time. This may easily be attributed to a lack of training and experience.

Note that the evidence is found at opposite ends of the house. This tells me that haste to flee was not a concern of the offender. These sketches were actually made at the scene in order to demonstrate the ease with which they could have been created.

THE GERMOND FAMILY MURDERS

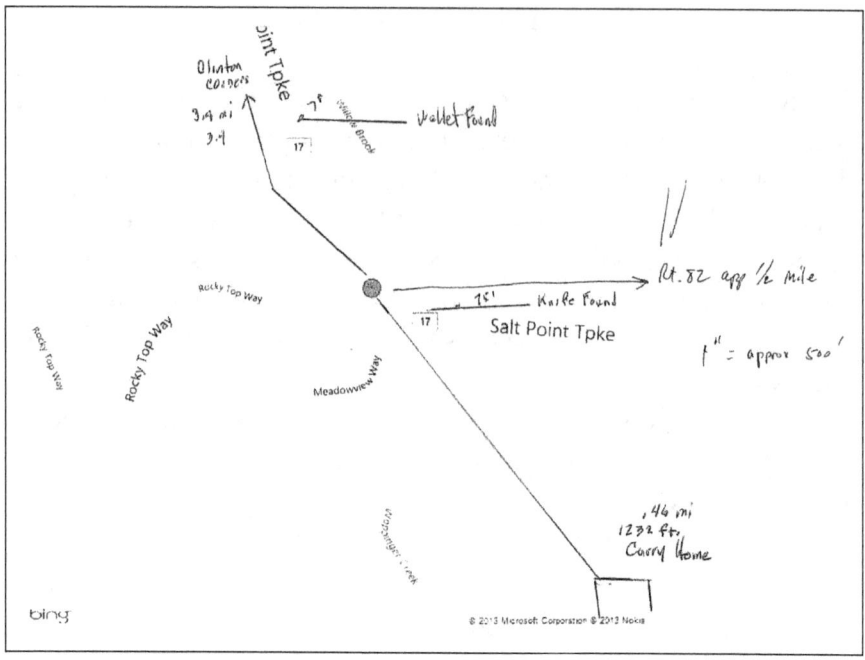

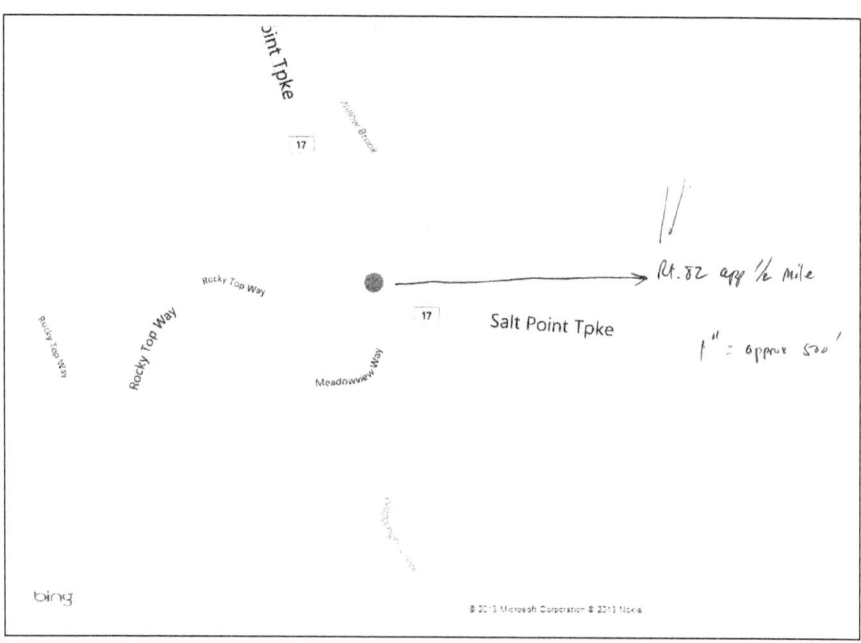

EXPLANATIONS & EXHIBITS

EXHIBIT #3 & 3A

This exhibit is a current photo of the Stanfordville Cemetery. The victims of this terrible crime rest approximately 75 feet from my family members. As a personal note; I knew these family members mostly in my childhood and adolescence. However, I have travelled the world over many times both in business and in the Marine Corps and I can honestly report that I have never encountered more wonderful people then my relatives who rest in this cemetery. I shall never forget them,

EXHIBIT #4

This is a current view of Oakleigh Robinson's store in Clinton Corners. It became famous for the ubiquitous "mystery man' who spent time in this store for about 2-3 hours after the crime and to whom it has been attributed virtually clairvoyant fetes.

This man was observed by at least four persons and none was able to observe any blood. In fact, he was dressed rather well and his "nice shoes" was commented upon – if he was the offender, he was certainly carrying a change of clothes with him.

The open area that he had to walk from the Germond house to this store could have provided ample opportunity for detection or observation as the numerous farm houses at this time had open visibility to the road. Moreover, he was observed at the store nearly three hours after the crime. He was a most casual multiple murderer less than 31/2 miles away. Where was he all this time? It seems as though the evidence indicates that he was a visitor to the area who told a major fib to get a ride.

EXPLANATIONS & EXHIBITS

EXHIBIT #5

This is the home of Arthur Curry. It is located .46 miles or 1231 feet from the crime scene. He was a local barber, former sheriff's deputy, chicken farmer and local raconteur. It is Mr. Curry who was convicted of this crime by rumor and inuendo by all including writers and would-be investigators. It should be noted that he has been convicted of other crimes unrelated to this matter. None of these amateur sleuths have ever seen the evidence in this case nor has any qualified person ever evaluated it. However, this enquiry has proven one old aphorism: "even a broken clock is right twice a day."

His home is within easy access to the Germond farm and its area is open to view from the road exactly as it was in 1930- I have walked to and from this location using various routes even across the field from the point where the wallet was found and the point where the knife was found. The longest route took me 6 ½ minutes. The various fetes attributed to Mr. Curry could have easily been accomplished in a minimum amount of time. His escape could easily have been unobserved.

EXHIBIT #6

This is a current view at the bridge over Wappingers Creek where a man confessed to over hearing the crime and observed some of it. This claim was dismissed without any documented evidence. My investigation conducted numerous tests and showed scientifically that this claim was invalid since it was virtually impossible.

Let us assume that the claimant mistook the bridge over Wappingers Creek for the overpass over Willow Brook. This is an even more absurd claim since the Willow Brook would not have facilitated concealment as the witness would have been virtually on top of the crime and easily visible to the offender. In addition, he got numerously disproven claims wrong.

The sounds created by the rushing waters of Wappingers Creek block even proximate sounds at that time of year. Numerous tests confirmed this.

EXHIBIT #7

Attached is a crime scene photo of the Germond residence. This photo has enormous significance in my ability to forensically opine on this case. The viewer will notice several significant issues such as the short distance from the side door (Salt Point Turnpike) and the front door and the very open space in the area in front of the side kitchen door. In short, this photo answers many questions and explains others as well as disproving a number of theories. Moreover, it proves that a passerby as well as a vehicle operator could easily observe most everything visible at this scene.

Obviously, the current scene has changed due to foliage and trees but not the visibility of the structures without ever entering on private property. At no time during this investigation did I or an assistant ever enter onto this property. There is unobtrusive technology that can be used for this purpose. It is this visibility that required the offender to remove the bodies from the yard knowing that the bus was coming and the bodies would certainly be visible and that he was the only person who could have known that the bus would stop in front of the house in order to let Bernice exit – accordingly he had no time to escape and she had to be killed.

EXPLANATIONS & EXHIBITS

EXHIBIT #8

The view in this crime scene photo shows the general location where a cab driver found the murder weapon at least a week after the crime had occurred. It demonstrates the level of competency of the investigators at the time. A perimeter search in the vicinity of a crime scene is a bare minimum activity for a crime scene investigator even in 1930.

Incidentally, Mr. Curry as soon as the crime was discovered, insisted on a perimeter search of the grounds for a weapon as he was persuaded that the offender brought the weapon to the scene and may have disposed of it nearby. How he could have discerned this must now be placed in the annals of clairvoyant forensics.

EXHIBIT #9

This crime scene photo shows a street level view (from the Salt Point Turnpike) of the crime scene and the distance between the wagon shed (far left) and the side kitchen door (far right). As can be demonstrated here is that a passerby both on foot or an operator of a vehicle could have easily observed activity in this area and most certainly would have observed two bodies lying in this yard. This photo must be considered of great probative value in this case. There is absolutely no evidence on the sworn record that the only vehicle seen in the yard was Mr. Germond's truck and there exists testimony to that effect.

EXHIBIT #10

This crime scene photo shows the front entrance to the wagon shed where the bodies of Husted and Raymond were found. Mr. Coons has testified under oath that the door was "slightly ajar" which is of great importance since there is evidence that a person other than Mr. Germond was observed seeming to "fix the door." The blood spatter can be clearly seen where Husted's body lay and was subsequently dragged into the shed.

THE GERMOND FAMILY MURDERS

EXHIBIT #11

This photo is not taken from the preserved crime scene photos. It was, however, produced by the technology found in the Dutchess County Clerk's Office and the assistance of Bradford Kendall, County Clerk, should not be underestimated. This reproduction clearly demonstrates the overview representing significant dimensions and distances that were essential in my final opinion in this matter. There is further commentary about these issues in the body of the book. The sites of the Germond House and the Curry residence are clearly seen as well as the distance.

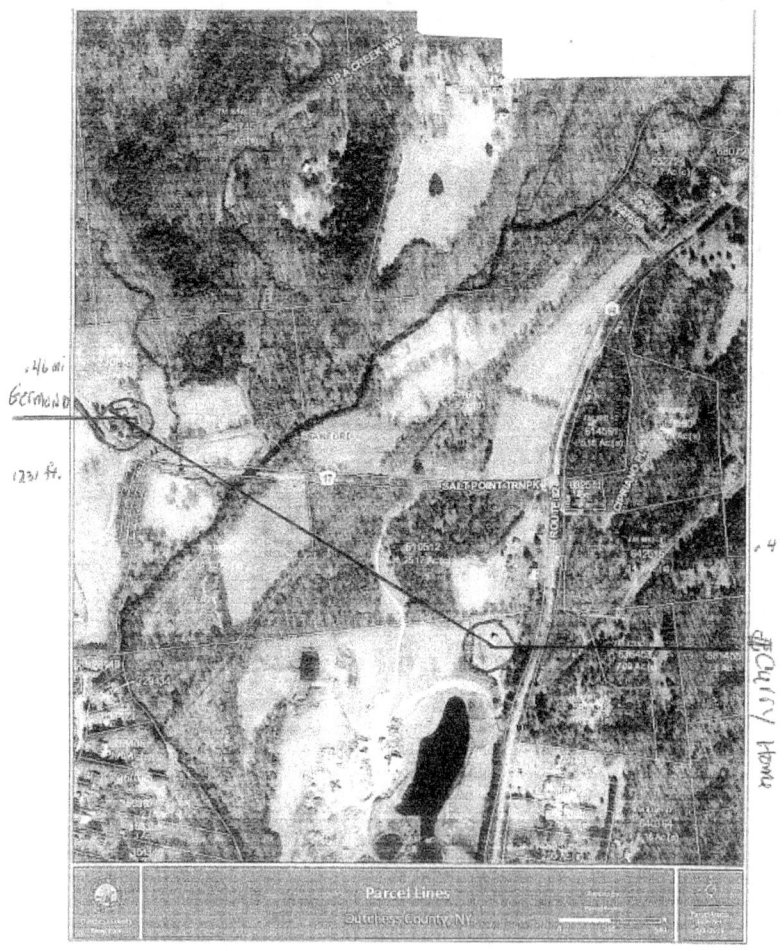

EXPLANATIONS & EXHIBITS

EXHIBIT #12 & 12A

These two crime scene photos are standing photos of Mr. Arthur Curry.

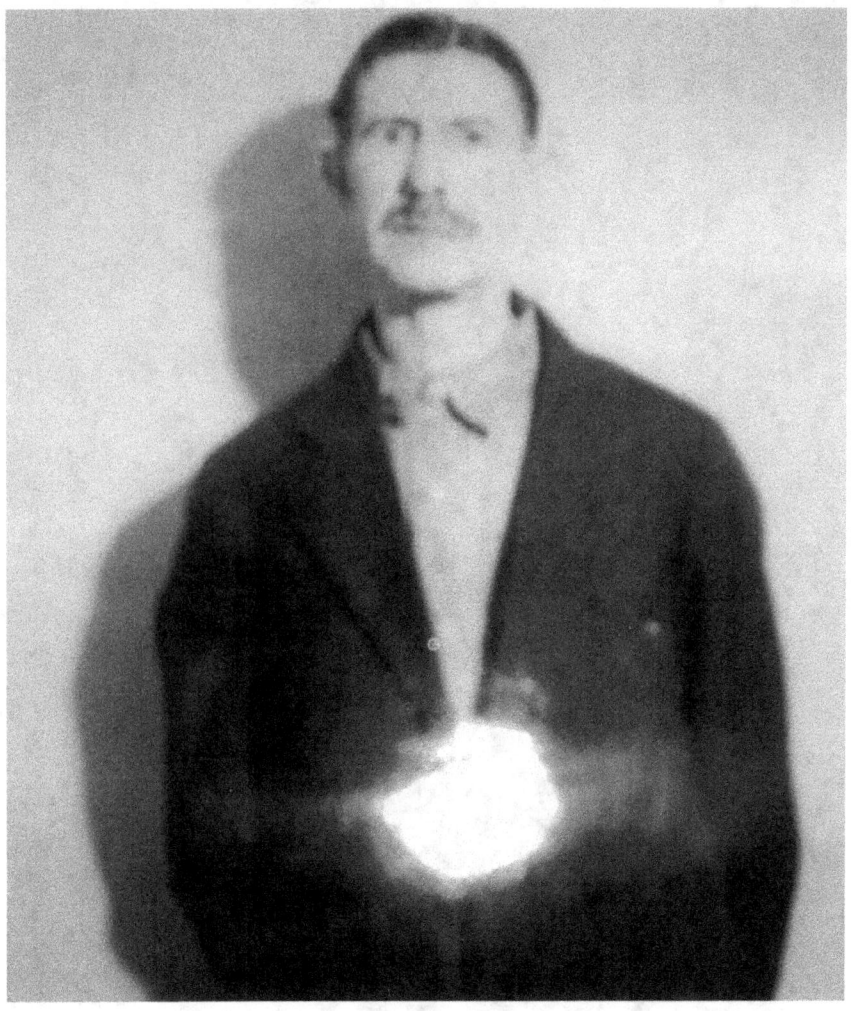

EXPLANATIONS & EXHIBITS

EXHIBIT #13

This crime scene photo is that of a newspaper laying on the table when Mabel and Bernice's bodies were found in the kitchen. Much has been made of this paper and some "investigators" over the years have used it to demonstrate that Bernice was sitting at the table reading when the intruder entered and began his attack.

I subjected this photo to extensive photographic examination and I was unable to prove the date of this newspaper and a search of the headlines was unsuccessful. Also, I was unable to obtain any cooperation from any newspaper publications. However, there is abundant evidence of great probative value to disprove this theory as was discussed in the book. I discontinued my search for the date of this newspaper due to the extensive timing needed and also that it was not truly significant in this case as the other evidence has indicated.

EXHIBIT #14

This crime scene photo depicts the famous brown gloves found on the table after the discovery of the crime. I have made some extensive commentaries in the book including the forensic photography used in the analysis that enabled me to opine on the endless investigation and speculation over the years about these gloves. The forensic evidence tends to indicate that the offender was in fact wearing these gloves.

One of the other crime scene photos of these gloves was of monumental significance. These gloves went uncommented upon for ninety years. This photo #22 provided a number of unexplained issues.

EXHIBIT #15 &15A

This is one of many crime scene photos of the murder weapon about which I make extensive commentaries. One of the photos contained visible plastic prints that I have analyzed and commented upon. Exhibit 15A is a photo of an exact match that I was able to obtain and trace to the exact manufacturer. It enabled me to conduct numerous forensic tests in order to demonstrate the assault and wounds.

There is a photo in a magazine depicting a man commenting over what he claims to be the murder weapon while standing in the Sheriff's Office. I have compared this photo with the actual weapon and they are decidedly different. This is a case of not only poetic license but also poetic construction.

EXHIBIT #16

View of the closed kitchen door taken several days after the crime. Note the exterior blood stains still visible outside the door.

EXHIBIT #17

View of door saddle with blood patterns clearly visible. Note the bottom of Mrs. Germond's shoe – very significant forensic crime scene photo, also note the bottom left foot of Mrs. Germond containing blood on the instep. This is forensic evidence of flight from outside the door after having been stabbed several times. No blood on the heel makes that conclusive. Also note the gravitational blood dropping on the step, door saddle, side of door and outside platform proving that the assault on Mrs. Germond happened initially in front of the side kitchen door. That Mrs. Germond stepped outside the kitchen is quite telling.

EXHIBIT #18

Close-up view of kitchen doorway and blood patterns. Note again bottom of the victim's shoe.

EXPLANATIONS & EXHIBITS

EXHIBIT #19

Mrs. Germond lying next to stove and blood stream from the area of her neck. My investigation reveals that this was falsely reported that she hit her head on the stove as she fell. Evidence reveals that her head was not injured and the blood reveals that she was still alive when she hit the floor. My subsequent review of Mrs. Germond's autopsy verifies my findings. The evidence indicates that she fell in flight from the kitchen doorway.

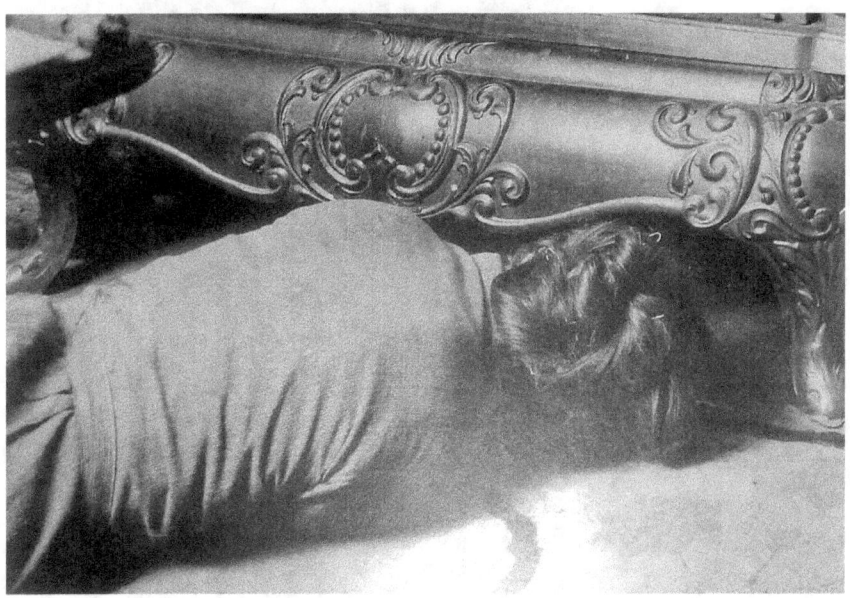

EXHIBIT #20

View of victim's body lying inside kitchen with body of Bernice in the distance under a table. This is a very significant crime scene photo. It is not only surprising but even shocking that no contemporary investigators drew any obvious scientific inferences from this photo. I make extensive commentaries in the book on this issue as it also tends to prove that the murder of Mrs. Germond and Bernice were two separate crimes as is evidenced by the gravitational blood patterns (discussed later).

EXHIBIT #21

Broader view of bodies in the kitchen. More definitive with respect to the blood patterns as well as subsequent autopsy protocols.

EXHIBIT #22

View of Bernice's body under table in kitchen. Many false forensic inferences were drawn from this photo. Extensive comments in the book. This photo is of great forensic value.

Please look carefully at this crime scene photo. Please note the gloves, which I have concluded were worn by the murderer, laying on the table near Bernice's body. This indicates, as the scientific evidence proves, that Bernice was killed last. If she was killed last, as the evidence proves, then this explains many of the unanswered questions in this case and point ultimately to a solution. Nowhere in the record is there any mention of this observation, yet it was absolutely crucial to a solution.

EXHIBIT #23

Closeup of Raymond's body in the shed offering some proof in the solution of this crime and completely refuting other theories over the years. It was quite cold outside at the time of this crime and Raymond is not wearing a jacket as would be the case working outside assisting his father. Even milk barns get quite cold as I can confirm. This is very persuasive evidence that Raymond came from the house to alert his father.

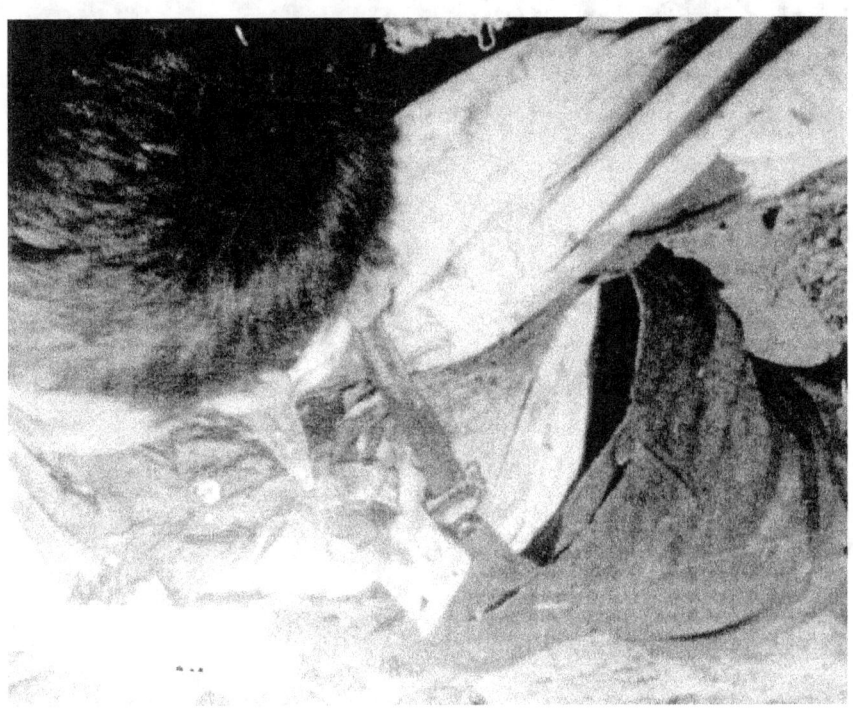

EXHIBIT #24

Hay wagon under which Raymond was "apparently" murdered – blood was found thereat.

EXHIBIT #25

View of the victim's bodies (Husted on left and Raymond on the Right) as they were discovered apparently having been dragged into the wagon shed from the site of their murders. Very important crime scene photo. Notice Mr. Germond is wearing a jacket and Raymond is not adding evidence to Raymond coming to alert his father. Very important issue in this photo. Note the blood in a descending flow from the top of Mr. Germond's head. This is not a usual wound from a stabbing. Mr. Germond's autopsy report was never found after a very extensive search. The head wound indicates to me one who has been struck in the head with the but of some object. It also states that Mr. Germond must have known the offender to permit such a close encounter and surprise attack.

EXHIBIT #26

View of the Germond farm the day after the bodies were discovered. This photo is all that one needs to demonstrate how not to handle a crime scene.

EXPLANATIONS & EXHIBITS

EXHIBIT #27

Less than one week after the crime, the first reward poster was issued.

SHERIFF'S OFFICE
DUTCHESS COUNTY
POUGHKEEPSIE, N. Y.

Identification Order
No. 103
December 10, 1930

$5,000.00 Reward

Wanted For Murder

The above reward is offered by the District Attorney of Dutchess County, New York, for the arrest and conviction of, or information leading to the arrest and conviction of the person or persons guilty of the murder of James Husted Germond, his wife Maybelle Germond, and their two children, Bernice Germond and Raymond Germond, whose bodies were found about 9:15 A. M., November 28th, 1930, on their farm at the Town of Stanford, Dutchess County, New York.

The murders were committed with a large butcher knife which was recovered. All the bodies bore numerous stab wounds, all being eventually stabbed in the heart. The father and son were found in the wagon house. The bodies of the mother and daughter were found in the kitchen of their home.

A billfold containing approximately eighty to ninety dollars was stolen from the body of James Husted Germond, the billfold being later recovered some distance from the scene of the crime.

It is urgently requested that every possible effort be used to apprehend the perpetrator of this deed.

V. J. ROCKEFELLER, *Sheriff*,
Poughkeepsie, N. Y.

WIRE ALL INFORMATION COLLECT TO:
JOHN R. SCHWARTZ, *District Attorney*,
POUGHKEEPSIE, N. Y.

THE GERMOND FAMILY MURDERS

EXHIBIT #28

Fingerprint card of Arthur Curry taken at Sing Sing State Penitentiary and used by me to compare patent prints on a knife.

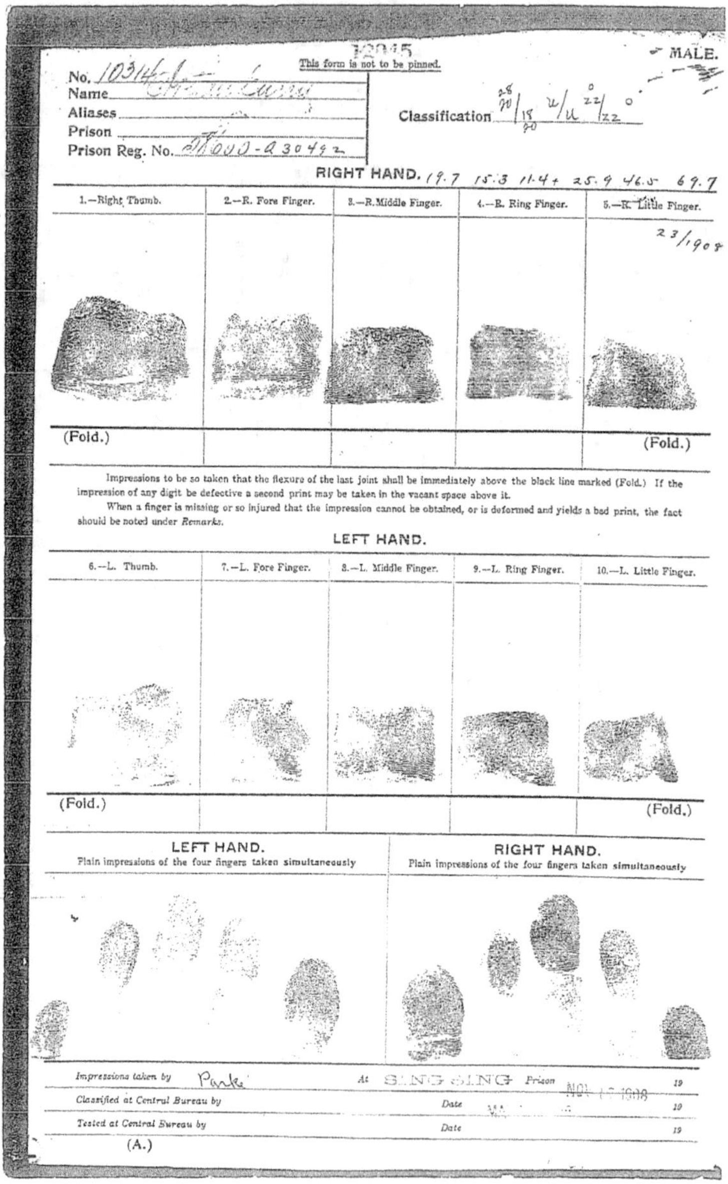

EXHIBIT #29

Death Notice Arthur Curry, Poughkeepsie Journal, Monday, January 3, 1955.

Poughkeepsie Journal Mon. 3 January 1955

Arthur Curry, Of Stanfordville

Arthur John Curry, 77, who had operated a pheasant farm in Stanfordville, died yesterday at his home after a long illness. Mr. Curry, who was a native of Ottawa, Can., had made his home in Stanfordville for 34 years.

Surviving are his wife, Mrs. Mary Tennant Curry, a son, Charles Curry, Framingham, Mass.; a daughter, Miss Anna Marie Curry, Stanfordville and a grandson Charles Curry Jr., Framingham.

* * *

FUNERAL SERVICES will be conducted at the home at 2 o'clock, tomorrow. The Rev. Harold Schaible, pastor of the Stanfordville Congregational church, will officiate. Burial will be in the Stanfordville cemetery under the direction of Peck and Peck. Bearers will be Eugene Sheldon, Harry Hall, John Battistoni Jr. and Richard Campbell. Friends may call at the home between 7 and 9 o'clock tonight.

ATTACHMENT # 36

EXHIBIT #'s 30, 30A, & 30B

Court Order signed by Supreme Court Justice, Christi Acker, authorizing my access to all the files and authority to proceed with my investigation. Also attached is a congratulatory letter from my attorneys. It should be noted here that since this crime in 1930, no other professional forensic scientist or competent investigator has ever been authorized to look into this very cold case. It is the belief of many professionals that I have solved it. The Court Order of Justice Acker was vigorously observed and no documents, exhibits, files, autopsy reports or any other information of any kind was published or provided to any person or entity.

NYSCEF DOC. NO. 15

INDEX NO. 2018-52380
RECEIVED NYSCEF: 01/18/2019

ATTACHMENT # 46-1
Germond Case 1930 49

> To commence the 30-day statutory time period for appeals as of right (CPLR 5513[a]), you are advised to serve a copy of this order, with notice of entry, upon all parties.

SUPREME COURT OF THE STATE OF NEW YORK
COUNTY OF DUTCHESS
--x
In the Matter of the Application of VINCENT P.
COOKINGHAM, Ph.D.,

For an Order Pursuant to New York County Law
§677(3)(b) Permitting the Dutchess County Clerk to
Make Medical Examiner Records Available for
Inspection by Forensic Scientist.
--x

ORDER PURSUANT TO
COUNTY LAW §677(3)(b)

Index No.: 2018-52380

Upon the Verified Petition of Vincent P. Cookingham, sworn to on the 2nd day of July 2018 and the exhibits attached thereto, and upon the admissions of service thereof executed by Dr. Dennis Chute, Dutchess County Medical Examiner (filed on August 20, 2018), Bradford Kendall, Dutchess County Clerk (filed August 20, 2018), Dutchess County Sheriff Adrian H. Anderson (filed on August 22, 2018), and Dutchess County District Attorney William V. Grady (filed August 14, 2018), and no opposition to the request for relief set forth in the Petition having been received by this Court,

NOW ON MOTION by McCabe & Mack LLP, attorneys for Petitioner, the Court hereby finds that pursuant to County Law §677(3)(b), Petitioner has established that he is a person with a substantial interest in the Dutchess County Coroner's records relating to the murder of the Germond Family which occurred on November 26, 1930, most particularly, the Inquest Minutes and the Coroner's Report. It is noted that Petitioner's application is supported by County Clerk Kendall, Sheriff Anderson and Medical Examiner Chute. District Attorney Grady indicates that

THE GERMOND FAMILY MURDERS

INDEX NO. 2018-52380
NYSCEF DOC. NO. 15
RECEIVED NYSCEF: 01/18/2019

he is neutral, but has no objection to the release of the records. Pursuant to the application before this Court, it appears that the records sought are in the sole possession of the Dutchess County Clerk. Accordingly, it is hereby

ORDERED that the Petition is GRANTED; and it is further

ORDERED that pursuant to County Law §677(3)(b), the Dutchess County Clerk shall make available to Petitioner for inspection and reproduction at his own expense, the Dutchess County Coroner's complete record of investigation and/or a transcript thereof regarding the Germond Family murder case occurring on or about November 26, 1930. This shall include the Coroner's Report and Inquest Minutes; and it is further

ORDERED that Petitioner may share the records received pursuant to this Order with the Dutchess County Sheriff's Office without further Order of this Court. Should Petitioner seek to share copies of said records with any other persons or entities, or should he seek to publish copies of said records, Petitioner shall submit a further application to this Court seeking permission to do so.

The foregoing constitutes the Decision and Order of the Court.

Dated: Poughkeepsie, New York
January 18, 2019

HON. CHRISTI J. ACKER, J.S.C.

To: All parties via ECF

ATTACHMENT # 46-2
Germond Case 1930 9

EXPLANATIONS & EXHIBITS

EXHIBIT #31

A copy of the letter from my attorneys congratulating me on this case. This firm represented me pro bono for historical purposes that the record may be completed on this historical case.

David L. Posner
Ellen L. Baker
Scott D. Bergin
Richard R. DuVall
Lance N. Portman
Richard J. Olson
Matthew V. Mirabile
Kimberly Hunt Lee
Rebecca M. Blahut
Daniel C. Stafford
Christina M. Piracci
Tristan Smith
Catherine Stefanik
Andrea L. Gellen
Cory A. Poolman
Sarah N. Wilson

Direct Dial: (845) 486-6858
E-mail: rduvall@mccm.com

McCM
McCABE & MACK LLP
ATTORNEYS AT LAW
mccm.com

Of Counsel
J. Joseph McGowan
Hon. Albert M. Rosenblatt
Hon. Ralph A. Beisner

John E. Mack 1874-1968
Joseph A. McCabe 1890-1973
Edward J. Mack 1910-1998
Joseph C. McCabe 1925-1981

ATTACHMENT # 48-2
Germond Case EXHIBIT # 31

January 23, 2019

vcooking@comcast.net
Vincent P. Cookingham, Ph.D.
676 Owl's Nest Court
Port St. Lucie, FL 34983

Re: Germond Case

Dear Dr. Cookingham:

It is a pleasure to finally provide to you the Decision & Order of the Hon. Christi J. Acker dated January 18, 2019. Also enclosed is our invoice for disbursements on this matter we handled on your behalf pro bono.

Should you have any questions, please do not hesitate to contact me.

Very truly yours,

McCABE & MACK LLP

/s/ Richard R. DuVall/
RICHARD R. DuVALL

RRD/kag
Enc.

63 Washington Street, P.O. Box 509, Poughkeepsie, NY 12602-0509 | 845-486-8900 | fax: 845-486-7621

www.ingramcontent.com/pod-product-compliance
Lightning Source LLC
Chambersburg PA
CBHW050104230526
45470CB00004B/1678